Also by Scott Dikkers

How to Write Funny

Welcome to the Future Which Is Mine

Trump's America: Buy This Book and Mexico Will Pay for It

You Are Worthless

The Pretty Good Jim's Journal Treasury

The Ascent of Plebes

*Destined for Destiny: The Unauthorized Autobiography
of George W. Bush*

The Onion's Our Dumb Century

The Onion's Our Dumb World

OUT RAGE OUS MARKETING

THE STORY OF THE ONION AND HOW TO BUILD A POWERFUL BRAND WITH NO MARKETING BUDGET

SCOTT DIKKERS

For the outrageous ones

Contents

1
THE LOVE ECONOMY

It was 3 a.m. The latest issue of *The Onion* newspaper was due to the printer in two hours, and I knew I wouldn't make the deadline.

The problem was page four. It was completely blank. I had nothing.

Local businesses paid serious money to place display ads with us. If we failed to publish, we'd be in violation of our insertion contract. We couldn't pay them back. We'd already spent the money.

If I couldn't make some magic happen and fill that space with something—anything!—we'd face financial ruin. *The Onion* would go bust.

It all fell to me, alone in the office, bleary-eyed from editing and laying out stories for more than 30 hours straight, trying desperately to get it done in time.

The strange thing is, as painful as this situation sounds, I was happy. Not because I'm a masochist or thrill-seeker, but because I had fallen in love.

Have you ever fallen in love?

I'm guessing you have.

I'm also guessing, since you're reading this, that you may have fallen in love with the same thing I did: *The Onion*.

If you have, you should know it's not weird. You're not alone. People tell me, "I love *The Onion!*" a lot. After someone meets me and finds out who I am, "I love *The Onion*" is usually the first thing they say to me.

Are you like those people? Has *The Onion* made you laugh at a time when you needed it? Was it there for you when life had you down and you needed a reminder not to take it so seriously?

If so, that's wonderful.

If you've fallen in love with *The Onion*, I hope it won't betray you to know that's exactly what I wanted you to do. I worked hard, over decades, trying to make you fall in love with it. In fact, what I was really trying to do was make you fall in love with *me*.

This is what performers do. They entertain you repeatedly and consistently until you love them. This is often what drives them. They got their first taste of applause or laughter when they were young and it made them feel loved. They wanted more.

The stories of creative people who make audiences fall in love with them could be written as a template. Just fill in the name: faced a troubled childhood, struggled to fit in, learned to be funny or entertaining as a way to get love, obsessively pursued a career in entertainment, faced setbacks, continued undaunted because of some deep emotional need, finally succeeded, earning the love of audiences everywhere.

This is a story like that. It's the story of *The Onion*, from the man who co-founded it, created its website, and helped make millions fall in love with its funny headlines and stories, its impossible photos, and its biting satirical point of view.

The Onion may not be a person you know. It may not be a beloved performer. But as a beloved comedy brand, *The Onion* occupies the same cultural space. Like a performer with a troubled past, *The Onion* is the repository of the inner struggles of several writers who, because of the circumstances of their family dynamics, school life, or early childhood experience, felt compelled to be funny.

I was one of them.

Comedians and comedy writers spend their lives and careers learning how to brand themselves, get attention, and get love by being funny. Most people who pursue comedy do it because they're funny people, or at least think they're funny. Most of them learned to be funny out of necessity, to mask life's pain, or to get validation. They adopted a funny outlook on life as a strategy for living. They self-medicated. Trauma, whatever form it took for them, provided fuel for a personal need and desire to make life more joyful. Their audience shares in that joy. But most people who succeed in comedy don't do it for the audience at the start. They don't do it to make money or to be famous. They do it to survive.

As a result, they develop tactics and strategies for bonding with people and winning them over. They develop these skills instinctively, naturally, and subconsciously. And they can be powerful. At times they're outrageous.

By building a fan base throughout their lives and careers, they become unwitting masters of their craft. They're the life of the party. They own every room they enter. When they speak, people are rapt. Audiences everywhere are poised to laugh and applaud.

In the same way, *The Onion* commands attention in a crowded media landscape. *The Onion* is a master distracter. In a world filled with distraction, this is no small achievement.

Every day we face the constant barrage of voices trying to get our attention. The stimuli comes from the multiple social-media apps on our phones, a thousand channels on TV, a billion websites, a trillion advertisements on billboards, in the sky, in malls, on people's T-shirts, on hats, in taxicabs, in movie theaters, in magazines, in newspapers, on receipts, on telephone poles. It's a 24/7 assault from every direction.

Getting people's attention is the commodity, or so we've been told. We live in an Attention Economy, they say. Marketing professionals are taught all kinds of tricks for grabbing people's attention: psychological techniques to take advantage of the human desire for instant gratification, linguistic tricks, certain sounds, flashing images, something eye-catching, something suggestive, the right combination of colors, maybe a celebrity cameo. Whatever the method, the repeated dopamine hits we get from something attractive and distracting are addictive, for both the consumer who feels them, and the marketer who spurs them.

But for the marketer, what good is getting someone's attention if you can't hold it? They're only going to get distracted by something else before they're done interacting with you.

The framing of "Attention Economy" is limiting. I believe we live in a Love Economy. People now want to spend their time, money, and attention on things they love, not simply things that grab their attention.

SEO is the right kind of marketing strategy in the Love Economy. It's more effective than "Hey, look at me! Look over here!" If someone is searching for something and we merely aim to be the object of their search, we're far more likely to succeed with them. They're already halfway to loving us. They want us; they just don't know it yet.

Branding, then, becomes a deeper and more meaningful pursuit in the Love Economy. Building a loyal fan base is a much more productive long-term strategy for selling products or services and creating a successful business. Haphazardly carnival barking at people as they pass by on the Attention Superhighway is the strategy of yesteryear.

This is a good thing. Love is better than mere distraction. No one wants to live in Aldous Huxley's dystopia where distraction blinds us from reality and turns us into mindless, consuming dullards. Love wakes us up. Love is fulfilling. And love is free—an important factor when you have no marketing budget.

The Onion is not a necessity. Nobody's going to die if it fails to deliver its humor and satire. But it's nonetheless figured out how to attract millions of readers, make millions of dollars, and make an impact in the world. *The Onion* succeeded by competing and winning in both the Attention Economy and the Love Economy. It succeeded by being outrageous, by making itself essential even when it didn't have to be.

And it did it without spending a penny on marketing.

I'm going to tell you how *The Onion* did it, how we grabbed attention and turned that attention into love. At the end, I'll sum up what I learned in a big-picture, actionable list. But first, the story.

2
AN IMPORTANT DISCOVERY

My little hand shook as I plucked the candy from the shelf and slipped it in my pocket. I felt the Chuckles package crinkle against my pant leg as I turned to walk out of the store. My legs wobbled beneath me. But somehow I propelled myself forward. An electricity surged through my slight frame. All my senses heightened. Time seemed to slow down.

I glanced furtively toward the registers. I noticed that particular smell of grocery-store produce as I passed apples laid out on purple cardboard at my eye level. On my way toward the automatic glass exit doors, the tinny sound of Musak began fading behind me. The bright light from outside and the freedom of the city lay before me.

The silhouette of a teenage clerk blocked my way. It towered over me.

"Are you going to pay for that?"

I searched for a lie. None came.

He gave me a knowing look.

"Come this way."

He put his hand on my shoulder and led me to one of those flapping plastic "employees only" doors on the other side of the small store. Once through it, he introduced me to a man in a necktie sitting behind a desk. They exchanged words, and then the two of them looked at me sternly.

My shoulder-length red hair probably hadn't been washed in days. My shirt was dirty and wrinkled like an old rag. I was barefoot, my feet blackened from the sidewalks.

The man with the tie asked to see what was in my pocket.

I lowered my head. My hand went into my pocket and slowly produced the Chuckles package. I held it out to him.

He took it and moved it around in his hand.

"Why'd you take the gumdrops, son?" He leaned in and raised his eyebrows. "Were you hungry?"

I knew what he was implying. I wasn't the homeless urchin he thought I was. In my imaginings I was just a normal kid.

I shrugged.

He stared at me in silence, waiting for a real answer.

The tension grew. He seemed to control it. The longer he sat and stared at me, the larger the pit in my stomach grew.

Tears burbled up. I couldn't stop them. Why was I crying? Not now, I urged myself. Play it cool!

But either way, no matter how I played this, I didn't know why I had taken the candy.

I was searching for something. But it wasn't Chuckles. I didn't know what I wanted. All I knew was that I wasn't finding it.

I had tried to find it months earlier when my younger brother and I ran away from home to live in a dead end just south of 50th Street that overlooked I-35W. We put as many of our belongings as we could carry in the weeds behind the curved crash barrier. We stayed there for hours, sustaining ourselves on peanut-butter-and-jelly sandwiches we'd brought.

Another place I looked was in the house of a family down the street. When they went on vacation, my older brother and I broke into their house by climbing into a window on the awning over their front door.

They had pennies everywhere—in ashtrays, jars, and under the sofa cushions. We took as many as we could and scurried home, thrilled to also find a few nickels and dimes in the mix.

One day I carried a raw egg down to the church on the corner of Nicollet and 49th street. One of the stained glass windows was open facing the alley. Toward the front of the church was a crowd of people dressed up, the men in black suits, the women in white dresses. One woman had a long white dress that everyone fussed over. They seemed so happy. Why did they get to have so much fun, I wondered?

I tossed the egg through the window and ran.

Things were going no better for me in my social life. I didn't know how to make friends. I was deathly quiet at school, especially after they tore down my neighborhood school and bussed me to a big experimental school closer to downtown. This school, Field Elementary, was more like a holding pen than a school. They threw all the kids together, fourth-through-sixth graders, regardless of age. I was the youngest. Every day an enormous and muscular sixth grader named Tony Jones would torment me. He'd take my lunch and threaten to beat me up after school. One day he brought a switchblade to school and showed it to me, promising he would stab me with it when I least suspected.

Other kids belittled me and laughed at me for being small, for looking poor, for having a pathetic peanut-butter-and-jelly-sandwich bag lunch—whatever they could think to say. I was an easy target who didn't fight back.

I cried a lot. I skipped school a lot. Life seemed pointless, unless I could find what I was looking for—a way out, a way to make sense of it, anything.

The man with the tie broke the silence. He picked up the phone on his desk and called the police. I sobbed uncontrollably. The sweat on my back made my shirt stick to the metal folding chair. I couldn't go to jail, I thought. I was only ten years old.

He held the phone to his chest and asked if I would prefer he call my mother instead.

Looking up at him, I searched his eyes. I saw myself in their reflection. He scraped the Chuckles package up and down against the five-o'clock shadow on his cheek, making a sound like sandpaper. The distinct whiff of aftershave mixed with body odor permeated his tiny office.

The tension became unbearable to me. I got up and ran as fast as I could through the "employees only" doors and out into the store.

The teenager called after me but I didn't look back. I moved my legs as fast as they could go. I tore out of the automatic doors as they opened for an old woman who was walking in. I bolted down the sidewalk and into the nearest alley. From there I shot between two garages and through a broken chain-link fence that I slipped through by bending it up from the bottom.

Like a feral cat I disappeared into central Minneapolis, which I knew well from my days skipping school and exploring.

But I didn't breathe easy. I could think only of how close I'd come to going to jail. I questioned the wisdom of my life. I wondered if I might still be caught. I wondered what would become of me if my parents ever found out what had happened.

I arrived home. No one was there. My mom was still at work. She was a receptionist at a hospital. My dad was gone, too, having left us months before.

I climbed the stairs and turned into my room. I locked the door behind me and sat on the edge of my ratty twin bed, trying to catch my breath.

That's how I'll do it, I decided.

I was done with all of it. There was nothing left to live for. I knew that if I couldn't breathe I couldn't live. In my thoughts, I said my goodbyes to my mom, my dad, my brothers, and my grandparents.

I sucked in all my air and held my breath for as long as I could.

The second hand on my wall clock got to the twenty-second mark before I reached my limit. I couldn't hold it any longer.

I tried again.

This time the second hand got to 20, then 25. I started feeling light headed. Is this what it feels before you die, I wondered? Things were getting serious. I kept holding it. 30. I could feel my face turning red. Would my head explode with blood? I had no idea. But the thought terrified me. I wanted to keep holding it but my desire to breathe was overpowering. My air came rushing out again and my lungs gasped.

My head hurt. I threw myself on my bed, cried, and pounded the pillow. Would nothing in this world go right for me? What joy was to be found? What meaning? It seemed a vast emptiness consumed me always. Whatever I was looking for, how could it possibly be found in this wasteland?

There was a possibility I had gotten close to discovering it years before. Cartoons I had drawn hung on my wall. I'd been drawing them ever since I can remember. A joke book I had written when I was five years old sat on my desk. My family didn't buy drawing paper, so it was made from scrap paper with printing on the back that my dad had brought home from his office. I had crudely stapled them together. It featured penciled jokes like "Why did't the sckeleten cras the road?" and then on the next page would come the answer: "He did't wan'to get raneoverd."

But my grandma seemed to like them. I made wall calendars for her, too, with a different drawing and a different joke for each month.

I pursued these creative labors without much thought. I was compelled to. I didn't know why. They just made me feel good. They gave me a chance to connect with other people, to communicate my thoughts and ideas. Drawing and writing in solitude was much easier than talking to people. And in return I got attention and praise, which I perceived as love and belonging.

I was far from the answers. In the pursuit of human connection, drawing funny pictures and writing jokes was one path I had taken, but it was unfocused and inadequate. I had no guidance. I didn't know how to harness it to find what I was searching for.

The store where I got caught stealing the Chuckles was several blocks from my house. I never went back there again. There were other stores near me. One was a dime store across from where my old school used to be.

I went to that dime store later that day, again looking for something. Maybe stimuli. Maybe something to get my mind off my life. Maybe the answers.

I didn't want to steal anything. I knew now that wasn't the right way for me.

I found myself passing the newsstand.

And there I discovered *Mad* magazine.

3
ART OR MARKETING?

I had found my place, my purpose, my position in the universe. I had found something to live for. It was comedy, and it came in the form of Alfred E. Newman sticking a finger up his nose. I didn't know it yet, but I hadn't just discovered comedy. I had discovered myself.

I studied *Mad*. It taught me how to draw better and how to write better. I imitated *Mad* artists like Don Martin, Sergio Aragonés, Jack Davis, and Mort Drucker.

Through a shared love of *Mad*, I became friends with Marcellus Hall, my first creative mentor. He was a year older than I was, had gone to Fuller Elementary School, and moved to Field Elementary where we were in the same class, since grades were mixed together. We frequently got together after school and on weekends to draw and act silly.

But for me our two-person *Mad* fan club wasn't just about comedy. It was a way to belong. It was a way to find an identity and to be some part—even a juvenile and contrarian part—of the larger community. I didn't know how to interact with people in the ways others did: making small talk, joining groups, and being chummy. These just weren't things I did. Marce helped me find my place.

Comedy was also a coping mechanism for me. It lifted me up when I felt alone or adrift. I used it to process the things that happened to me: bullies, my parents' divorce, simply being an awkward kid who didn't seem to fit in anywhere. I used comedy to lash out at the world, but also to make sense of it.

Marce was a spectacular artist. His cartoons as a fifth grader looked like the work of a professional illustrator. Beyond his drawing skill, he used comedy as a way to express his skepticism of adults and society at large. He kept me sharp by questioning assumptions and being painfully honest.

Mad's competition at the time was *Cracked*, and Marce and I had chosen our tribe. We were *Mad* fans. *Cracked*, we decided, sucked.

One day Marce drew two single-panel cartoons. He showed them to me and asked what I thought. They were drawn amazingly well, of course, and the jokes were solid, so I told him I thought they were great.

"Got ya!" he said.

Then he revealed that had copied the jokes directly from *Cracked*, proving to me that our professed hatred of the much-maligned humor magazine was unfounded.

I produced more joke books. I bought small spiral notebooks at the dime store and drew cartoons and stories in them, usually with ballpoint pen, then coloring them with a set of Marvy Markers I'd gotten for Christmas. I made ABC books primarily, with a different single-panel joke for each letter. Most of them featured a recurring character I named "Gus Hooper" who wore a red-and-white striped shirt and blue pants. One book was the story of Gus Hooper's family history, where the character's ancestors who looked just like him appeared in various important historical periods. Booker T. Hooperton, for example. The character looked a lot like Waldo, ten years before the first *Where's Waldo* book (there's no relation).

I also created books of character archetypes, showing off my versatile style with drawings of different people: an artist, a thief, a mad scientist, a tourist, and several others. I made a book using news magazine cutouts instead of drawings, with straight-faced captions as if it were a serious biography. I made a "reveal the drawing" book, inspired by one of Marce's projects, where every other page of the notebook was cut in half, which made a different picture when you flipped up the half page. It was like a poor kid's *Mad* Fold-in.

Marce's and my comedy aspirations began to bleed into other media, inspired by the tear-out vinyl 45s that sometimes came in *Mad*. We used a cassette-tape recorder to produce comedy skits. Marce was a gifted voice actor with great comic timing. We created a fake game show, a fake soap opera, and "Funny Fone Calls," a series of short vignettes where we acted out imaginary phone pranks.

Later, we conducted actual phone pranks, calling random people from the phone book and pretending to be radio DJs giving away money.

The fun came to an end when my mom remarried an abusive alcoholic named Jerry Keilas who had the crazy, romantic idea to move to a hobby farm in Ellsworth, Wisconsin.

Whereas in Minneapolis I could skip school and explore the city all day, on the farm there was no escaping the bus to school, or Jerry's strict discipline. Before school every morning, I now had to get up at 4 a.m. to feed the chickens, the pigs, the cow, and the horse. On weekends I had to clean the chicken coop, the pig pen, the horse's stall, and the cow's stall. I had to mow the five acres of grass on the farm. In the winter my brothers and I put on our snowsuits and spent weekends chainsawing firewood from land that wasn't ours. Jerry would drink brandy in the heated comfort of the station wagon while we trudged through deep snow loading stolen logs into the trailer, our fingers and toes frostbitten.

For about a year, in a new school with all new bullies, I retreated into myself and used what little time I had for creative work to write letters and send drawings to Marce. He would inspire me with everything he sent back. Our letters got sillier and sillier. We started sending cassettes to each other, complete with sketches and comedy bits. "Mail tapes," we called them.

Soon enough, I gathered comedy cohorts in Ellsworth. My junior high-school classmates Vincent Taylor and Mark Leonard and I formed an imaginary show called "The Dick Vince and Len Show." We used a sound effect record I had with a laugh track on it to craft a comedy routine on cassette that perfectly matched the pauses and intensity of the laughs on the record to make our recording sound like it had a real live audience.

In school we competed for the mantle of class clown, getting together like stand-ups at the Comedy Cellar after a show, recalling which ad-libs had killed that day in class.

One day, when one of our teachers was late, I stood in front of the class and performed an improvised stand-up routine, doing my best impression of the teacher, holding the class's attention for several minutes.

I also learned to juggle. I practiced all summer, perfecting tricks and building a little routine. I found a ride to the International Jugglers Convention in Cleveland, Ohio, when I was 16. There I met TV star Peter Scolari, better known as Tom Hanks' buddy on *Bosom Buddies*. He was on top of the world, starring in a hit sitcom. We passed clubs (that's when two people juggle clubs between them). I also met eight-year-old Anthony Gatto, a wunderkind from a juggling family who could already juggle seven rings. He performed on stage at the convention, which impressed me. I didn't perform—I didn't even know how you signed up to do that. I taught him how to throw a plunger on the floor so that it would stick. As an adult he would become widely recognized as the greatest juggler in the world.

I began writing comedy stories in high school, fanciful one-pagers written by hand that mostly used dramatic story structure—the opposite of what I would later do at *The Onion*. I wrote these as a kind of writing practice, but others read them and seemed to enjoy them. I wrote one of them in Diane Hines' yearbook. She gave it to me to sign, even though I barely knew her and spent no time with her. The expectation was that I would say "have a nice life" or whathaveyou, but I wrote page after page after page of fake reminiscences in the margins. She seemed amused by the irony.

I crawled to school one day with my friend Troy Whipple. People couldn't stop talking about this particular stunt. For years after we were known as "the kids who crawled to school." Crowds gathered. Someone called the police. In the end we weren't charged with anything; they couldn't come up with any law we were breaking besides just being strange. The townsfolk probably still tell stories about this.

When I was a teenager I sometimes called radio stations and pretended to be the president. Sometimes they put me on the air. One day around 1984 I called AM station KSTP in Minneapolis–St. Paul during a listener-call-in show about personal finance. They enjoyed my performance and kept me on the air to answer calls from listeners. One caller actually believed I was Ronald Reagan.

Getting attention was something I was getting good at.

Again inspired by Marce, I started drawing a comic strip for the school newspaper with the same name as a comic strip he was drawing for his school newspaper: "Noah Spirit." It was an easy comic for me to write since I loathed the idea of school spirit. Noah was a grumpy character who bemoaned pep rallies or any positivity in school life. The comic strip went on to win first prize in a statewide journalism contest. One of my teachers had entered it. Apparently there was a gala award ceremony put on by the sponsor, a major Milwaukee newspaper. I didn't get word about the ceremony but they mailed me a nice plaque.

The thing I had been searching for was coming into clearer focus. I didn't go to parties in high school. I didn't drink. I was still deeply uncomfortable in any social setting. Much as I may have thought life would be better if I could just hide under my covers all the time, humans are social creatures. We thrive on making social connections, and I needed that as much as anyone else. But I wasn't comfortable doing it the normal way. The way I had grown up and the way I had forged a place in society was through comedy. Instead of interacting with people and talking to them as friends, I connected by making things that made them laugh. That interaction made sense to me. Hanging out with people and talking about the weather or gossip didn't make any sense to me. Most of my friends were just glorified co-workers. I didn't spend time with them unless we were writing or recording or drawing.

I had discovered an extreme introvert's workaround for fulfilling the basic human need for community.

As I was producing comedy on paper, on audiocassette, and on stage—makeshift or otherwise—another means of connecting with people was brewing. And it would one day take over my life.

Jaws came out in the summer of 1975 when I was in fifth grade. It played at the Boulevard Theater in Minneapolis, which I could walk to from my house. The movie made me jump out of my seat in terror.

Two years later my dad took me to a midnight showing of *Close Encounters of the Third Kind*. I was inspired and awestruck by the possibility that space aliens could make contact with humans.

What I didn't realize at the time, and what would strike me with even more awe later, was that these two movies had come from the mind of the same person.

Raiders of the Lost Ark came out when I was in high school. It fueled my adrenaline and my imagination like no other action movie had. *E.T.* followed a year later. I sobbed like an infant at *E.T.*

By my junior year in high school, I was captivated by Steven Spielberg's mastery of a peculiar craft: connecting with people emotionally and making them feel however he wanted.

I was further captivated when I learned that he'd been an awkward kid, a misfit who got bullied. He was like me, I imagined. He struggled with the same problems. He had solved his by becoming a master storyteller. He could command an audience's attention and hold it. He connected with people on a deeper level than I did. I knew how to do it with jokes, but I had no other tools. It didn't escape my attention that, conversely, Spielberg seemed inept in the one category I felt I was mastering: comedy. *1941*, his first comedy, was a major flop.

I branched out and began making movies on super-8 film, trying to summon my own Spielbergian magic. One of my movies was about an incompetent superhero. He was Electron Man, and he battled an alien super villain (played by my brother Alan) and ended up losing the climactic battle and being framed for a petty theft unrelated to the story. It was *Mad* magazine meets Spielberg.

My other big film production in high school was *Bird Man*, the story of a birdwatcher who's obsessed with birds, his head constantly buried in ornithology books. He finds what he believes is a rare white feather while lost in the wilderness and looks for the bird it belongs to. He emerges in a clearing and discovers the source of the white feather: several specimens of a strange bird nowhere to be found in his birdwatching handbook. He believes he's discovered a wondrous new species, and is convinced he's destined to become the greatest birdwatcher of all time. In fact he has merely stumbled upon chickens in a barnyard. He takes pictures of the birds to document his find, only to learn later, after he's left the scene, never to find it again, that he accidentally left his lens cap on.

One of the bit players in that movie, a farmhand who paused for a moment bailing hay to observe the strange birdwatcher, was a theater student at nearby UW–River Falls named Mike Nelson. He would later become the host of the cult TV series, *Mystery Science Theater 3000*.

To score *Bird Man*, I used canned music from John Williams' score from both *Jaws* (the other parts, not the famous shark-attack part) and *Close Encounters* (to evoke a sense of awe for the chickens).

My new friend Keith Webster and I made movies together. Keith's movies were more polished. He was a few years older than I was and had actually gone to film school. So, he knew about things like white balance and focus.

One of Keith's best movies was an eerie short called *Due Date*, about a mysterious character who walks through the city to mesmerizing and creepy music, then reacts to a headline in a newspaper dispenser on the street: "Librarian Murdered, Reason Unknown." He walks to a foggy lake, takes a book out of his pocket, flips open the front cover, and we see the library tag stamped "overdue." He throws the book in the lake, then he throws a gun, and then walks off.

Keith and I wrote a lot of scripts, not just for movies, but for comedy radio plays, which we also produced with the help of our mutual friend Peter Hilleren. Keith and I would typically write the scripts. We would then go to Peter's parents' palatial hilltop country estate to record them on his expensive cassette stereo system. He had microphones and sound effect records and everything. I brought mine too. We also created a lot of our own Foley effects.

We developed several radio-drama series. One was a parody of *Buck Rogers* called *Mr. Average*. He was a regular Joe from the 20th century who somehow became a superhero because he had been thrust into the 24th century, which was our beef with the actual *Buck Rogers* story. It never made sense why he was a hero; he was just an average guy in a different time. We wrote and produced several half-hour episodes of that show. My brother Alan starred as Mr. Average.

Another show was *The Great Adventure Series*, a parody of a genre that may not exist, that of privileged American plutocrats going on adventures to the far corners of the globe. This was a Zucker-brothers-style goof-fest packed with ridiculous antics and absurd madcap. Keith, Peter, and I played all the parts. John Williams' bombastic *Raiders of the Lost Ark* music scored "The Amazon Adventure." Lawrence Rosenthal's music from the original *Clash of the Titans* was used for the next episode, "The Himalayan Adventure," in which our heroes embark on a quest to have a picnic on the peak of Mount Everest.

Besides sound-effect records, movie soundtracks were the only other genre of record I bought.

Our most prominent series was *John Smith, Private Eye*. Smith was an incompetent private detective from the 1940s, similar to the Pink Panther. But unlike the Pink Panther, John Smith didn't miraculously solve cases by accident. He bungled them as a true incompetent private investigator would. So, the ending of the show was often just him standing befuddled by the disaster he'd made of the case. Yet he had a grand opinion of his sleuthing skills.

This "bumbling authority" archetype, a low-level authority figure who blusters with self-importance but is actually a fool, is one I would come back to many times in my career.

We wrote and produced no fewer than six half-hour episodes of *John Smith, Private Eye*, and used brooding Maynard Ferguson bigband jazz to set the mood for his Mickey Spillane-style narration.

Keith made a film based on Smith, adapting the first show we had produced in the series, an improvised story about the incompetent John Smith confronting a fitting arch enemy—an incompetent killer. I played the killer, a sweaty, clearly guilty murderer who tried to throw off police by adopting the poorly thought-out alias, Charlie Upthestreet.

Keith also wrote poetry, painted, and drew cartoons. He was a creative powerhouse, unlike any other person in the small farm town of Ellsworth. He had already graduated high school by the time I entered. But we got together frequently, obsessively producing media.

We experimented in less-traveled media as well. We created street art akin to my crawling-to-school stunt. While other kids in town were driving their muscle cars blaring Kiss or Van Halen, Keith and I drove down Main street in Ellsworth at midnight blasting a dainty wind quintet from public radio at full, speaker-thumping volume while hooting like crazed heavy-metal fans.

No one called the police that time.

One day we volunteered to be clowns in a parade promoting a local candidate for district attorney. I juggled. We made bad puns and experimented with meta-humor.

On Halloween one year we created a haunted house. It was an attempt to elevate the idea of the haunted house beyond simple toilet-paper roll and pipe-cleaner bats on pulleys, or people in mediocre costumes popping out from dark corners to spook patrons. Our goal was to create an experience of true psychological horror, a meta-haunted house. When visitors came into the basement where we'd staged the affair, our plan was to pretend there was an argument among different members of the haunted-house crew. There would be a staged falling out, a heated, violent breakup that would end in most of the group storming out. The one who remained would seem unhinged, and would hold the visitors in a locked room like hostages, telling them he was going to torture them to death to get back at his fellow haunted-house creators who had wronged him. We wanted to make trick-or-treaters feel genuine fear.

We ended up having an actual falling out with the others involved, and our plan never came to fruition. But Keith and I disguised ourselves and went through the haunted house pretending to be out-of-control residents of a nearby halfway house, making our friends nervous and uncomfortable.

Keith was a kindred spirit. While it seemed everyone else in our age group in Ellsworth was spending their time cruising, getting drunk, getting pregnant, or all of the above, he and I didn't have social lives or dating lives. We were creatives. There was no one else like us in town. He was a godsend to me—literally; we originally met in church. I don't know what would have become of me had I not had Keith as a kind, patient, and accomplished mentor, an excuse for me to justify my insatiable thirst to create media and entertainment. High school years can be traumatic when you don't interact socially with other people the way everyone else does, but Keith gave me a different path.

I've never considered myself an artist. Keith, however, studied art in college and painted abstract paintings. He respected art. I didn't. Art confused me. It still does. What is the point of it? The point of entertainment is clear: an emotional reaction from the audience. This is a more visceral and satisfying way to connect with people. Art is beautiful sometimes, but more often than not it seems meant to confound audiences with highfalutin meaning. To me a well-crafted piece of comedy that makes a lot of people laugh is more beautiful. But in my mind this fact still doesn't mean comedy is art. It's entertainment. Art is for elitists; entertainment is for everybody.

Spielberg understood this. He wasn't making artistic films meant to dazzle the critics or win awards (at least, not at first). He was making popcorn movies to appeal to the widest possible audience. I respected that. I believed it was a higher calling—a more important one than mere art.

What I didn't put together at the time was that this pursuit of an ever-larger audience to delight and connect with is the same thing advertising tries to do.

I've never met Steven Spielberg, but as a teenager, I felt like I knew him. People like Spielberg and me used entertainment to get people's attention and love. Most people didn't need to do this because they liked hanging out with friends and going to parties and other normal things. But Spielberg and I didn't bond with people like that, I believed. We bonded by making things, telling stories, and cracking jokes.

Life was an Attention Economy and a Love Economy, and I was baking skills into my introverted personality to get attention and love. Without realizing it, I was learning an extremely effective form of marketing.

4
AN OUTRAGEOUS COMIC STRIP

By the time I got out of high school, I had already logged several years as a practitioner of the as-yet unknown marketing principle I've now coined "Outrageous Marketing." I obsessively produced content that was crafted to get people's attention and make them love me, and I did it because I needed to for my emotional survival.

But I hadn't made any money. That would be the real test.

At 18, the only plan I had to succeed in the entertainment business was to create a brilliant comic strip like Cathy Guisewite had. I'd send it unsolicited to a major syndicate just like she had. They'd be so blown away by its quality that they'd send me a lucrative contract in the mail to draw cartoons for major newspapers, just like her, and I'd be set.

My plan was to do this immediately after graduating from high school.

That plan derailed when I flunked out of high school.

In my senior year I signed up for study hall for the first two hours of every day. I did this so I could stay up late to watch *Late Night with David Letterman* and then sleep in. I would show up at school around 10 a.m.

The assistant principal, Mr. Molitor, sat me down in his office and explained that this bastardization of the schedule wasn't acceptable.

"It's acceptable to me," I said, feeling an adrenaline surge from daring to disagree with an authority figure.

He rubbed his temples.

"All students are required to arrive at school by the starting bell."

"So, you want me to come in and sit in a study hall for two hours and do nothing when I could be home sleeping?"

"Yes. That's what I'm telling you."

I huffed.

"Well, that doesn't work for me."

"Alright, you're going to be suspended then."

"Okay, wonderful."

My passion to produce entertainment was all that mattered to me. I didn't care about following rules. The three-day suspension was a nice break. I used it to write and draw.

When I returned I had gained no favor with Mr. Brown, the overtly religious math and computer teacher who quoted from the Bible a lot in class. He told me I was going to get a failing grade. Looking back, I can't understand why he would give a student like me an F in math or computers. While it's true I did poorly in math, I made up for it by spending nearly every day after school in his extra-credit computer lab.

The previous year the school had purchased three Apple IIe computers, one of the earliest personal computers for sale to consumers. I learned to program them using Basic, and I made video games and interactive animated stories. They were quite elaborate, and the other students loved them.

This extracurricular passion should've counted for something, but Mr. Brown failed me anyway. In retrospect, I imagine it was the bad reputation he felt I'd earned from the suspension coupled with the fact that whenever he quoted from the Bible, I let him know after class that this was a public school and he was in violation of the First Amendment.

It didn't matter that he failed me. I knew I wouldn't be pursuing math. I would be pursuing comedy. And when they hired for comedy jobs, I reasoned, they didn't ask to see your high-school diploma. They only cared if you were funny.

But then I was saddled with the task of figuring out how to make a living doing comedy.

I had no way into the business. My family had no connections. We were poor. We lived in the middle of nowhere. There was no Internet, so the road map for succeeding in such an unusual profession wasn't something you could just Google. In those days and in that part of the country, there were three possible trajectories for a young person's career: get an unskilled minimum-wage job, go to vocational or technical community college to get a blue-collar job, or go to a university and hope to get a white-collar job.

I searched the town library. They had only one book that was even remotely related to the subject of the entertainment business: *How to Be a Ventriloquist*.

I checked out the book, of course, and read it, just in case there was anything useful in it. There wasn't.

Faced with no prospects, I did the only thing I knew: I drew cartoons. I decided to pursue my Cathy Guisewite plan. I drew a cartoon that I thought was funny and professional and suitable for major newspaper distribution. It was called "Melon Man," and it featured a parody of a superhero character. He was big and muscular and had super powers, but he was lazy and just sat around all day. Syndicate editors roundly rejected it.

The next cartoon idea I hatched was "Chester." Chester was a polar bear and the comic strip was a sitcom about him and his family. It was like "For Better or Worse" but with polar bears. Chester met the same fate as Melon Man.

I was undaunted. I was going to be a professional cartoonist, I decided. These big syndicates just didn't know it yet.

A source of my confidence was a series of books by Ken Muse I'd discovered at a bookstore in Minneapolis. They were exactly what I needed, exhaustive instructions for how to draw and sell cartoons to make a living as a cartoonist: *The Secrets of Professional Cartooning* and *The Total Cartoonist*. Muse became an important mentor to me, albeit in book form.

One of the best nuggets of advice he offered, beyond all the practical advice on how large to draw the cartoons and what kind of Bristol board to draw them on and other such details, was to take pride in rejection letters. He recommended hanging them on the wall and celebrating them. Some people might quit after one or two ideas are rejected, but he knew the important thing was to keep trying. It was brilliant advice.

The dumb confidence of youth is a critical ingredient for early success in life. It's like rocket fuel. For a rocket to break out of Earth's atmosphere it needs to burn an incredible amount of fuel. Once it achieves orbit, its own inertia does the work, so it doesn't need fuel anymore. Youthful idealism and confidence is like that initial burst of rocket fuel. When we're young and hungry and feel like we can conquer the world, we burn this fuel not realizing how unlikely our chances of success are. But if we get lucky, if we get a foothold on our goals, we can rely on a little bit of inertia. It's more difficult to succeed starting at zero when you're older, when you don't have that youthful confidence anymore. You may not believe in yourself as much because you've faced too much stark reality, so you don't quite have enough fuel to break out.

After spending several years drawing cartoons and sending them to syndicates unsuccessfully, I finally got a job. At McDonald's. Despite my best efforts, I had embarked on the first of the three possible trajectories for a young person's career: an unskilled minimum-wage job.

Working at McDonald's, which I did full time for almost two years, was a good experience for me. It taught me how to run a business, it taught me a work ethic, and it taught me some minimal social skills.

The crew at the McDonald's where I worked, in Madison, Wisconsin, was tightly knit, and they accepted me as part of their little community.

In every spare moment that I wasn't working at McDonald's, I continued to draw cartoons. I had no friends. I had no social life outside of work. But I was starting to feel like my rocket was spinning in circles. So, instead of working hard, I decided to begin working smart.

The Madison Public Library had a book that listed every newspaper in America. I painstakingly retyped every address from that book onto address labels. I created a comic strip called "Urban Blight," a single-panel cartoon about 9-to-5 life in a modern city, and sent out copies of the cartoons to every newspaper.

A tiny handful of the hundreds of newspapers that I had contacted agreed to run my cartoon on a weekly basis. One of them, the *LA Downtown News* in Los Angeles, paid me $40 per comic. The others paid around $10. This wasn't enough money to live on, but it was the foothold I needed.

One of the student newspapers at the University of Wisconsin–Madison, *The Daily Cardinal*, held a twice-yearly meeting that any student could attend. Even though I wasn't a student, I showed up, figuring they would never check to see if I had a student ID. A local cartoonist who had made it big, John Kovalic, was at this meeting holding court and offering advice to wannabe cartoonists. His daily comic strip, "Wildlife," ran in *The Cardinal* for years and had been picked up by Chronicle Features, a major syndicate. He also self-published a book collection of his comics.

This meeting is where I first saw Todd Hanson, a UW student who would later become the head writer of *The Onion*. He approached John with the large originals of a comic strip he had created, "Badgers and Other Animals." He showed it to him, his hands shaking. He complimented John on all his success, expressed how inspirational "Wildlife" had been to him, and asked for advice.

John complimented Todd's work and critiqued his drawings. Todd used an extra-fine Sharpie to draw his cartoons, not a quill pen like professionals were supposed to use. However, he drew his lines in varied widths so as to appear like they'd been drawn with a quill pen. It was detailed work. John was impressed, but advised Todd to learn to use a quill pen.

I didn't speak to anyone at the meeting. I was there for one reason: to submit a new comic strip I had created, an experimental piece of work called "Jim's Journal," to Keith Doherty, the newspaper's graphics editor. He wasn't impressed with the minimal text or affected stick figures I used, but he agreed to run the strip on a trial basis every other day to see if people liked it.

"Jim's Journal" was an unusual comic strip. Most people didn't understand it at first. There were no traditional gags and the art was purposefully crude (I used a thick Sharpie and didn't vary my line widths). Its humor came from a subset of meta-humor I would later dub "anti-humor." It was a parody of mainstream comic strips, which I thought were hackneyed as a rule. It was subtle and quiet. Each comic was the daily journal of the lead character, Jim. He simply told readers what he did that day, as if he wrote the comic himself.

Jim was a soft-spoken, existential character who didn't have strong opinions and didn't write about anything important. Readers saw only the small in-between moments of his and his friends' lives. He had blasé catchphrases like "It was okay," and "It was pretty good." With a comic strip about nothing a year before *Seinfeld*'s debut, I was tapping into the slacker vibe of Generation X at the time.

Artistically, the comic achieved everything I believed comic strips were meant to achieve: it was easy to read, it was drawn simply so it popped off the page, and it had recurring characters that were clear archetypes that readers could look forward to seeing every day and eventually fall in love with. This last feature is where "Jim's Journal" had a leg up on the competition. Readers could get to know Jim on a deeper level than they had known comic strip characters before, because he wasn't just telling jokes; he was telling people about his life. The humor came from readers recognizing themselves in Jim and the other characters. The first-person narration of the strip, which was not used in newspaper comics at the time, made it even more intimate. It also made it feel fresh and original.

A few weeks after my trial period, Keith decided the strip was doing well enough to justify running it daily. This meant I would be paid the standard rate for a cartoonist in *The Daily Cardinal*: five dollars a week.

I felt like I had finally achieved some success drawing comic strips. But I still didn't make enough money to pay rent. I bounced around day jobs. I parlayed my many years producing audio into an entry-level position at the local public radio station, where I edited tape and pre-answered calls for call-in programs.

In time "Jim's Journal" started building a fan base. I started selling Jim T-shirts at a local T-shirt shop. They became extremely popular. Since the strip was succeeding in Madison, I thought it might succeed on other college campuses too. I found another book in the library that listed all the college newspapers in the country. I did the same thing I had done with "Urban Blight." I sent "Jim's Journal" comics to every college newspaper. But this time, instead of just sending some strips with a letter explaining the submission, thanking the editor for their consideration, I provided paste-up ready "Jim's Journal" comics with a one-sheet describing the success it was enjoying in Madison. *The Daily Cardinal* happened to be one of the largest and most widely respected college newspapers in the country. So, this was a selling point.

But I didn't stop there. I continued to send the comic every week, like clockwork, as if the newspaper had already signed up to run the strip.

I had seen how college newspapers operate. Often the editors are students who don't put the time or effort necessary into planning. So, sometimes they just need stuff to fill space when they're up against a deadline and don't have enough stories. I was pushing the envelope with an outrageous strategy that, as far as I knew, no one had yet tried: simply sending newspapers my comic for free.

Another thing I'd learned about the comic strip business from Ken Muse is that it's very difficult for a newspaper to stop running a comic strip that's popular. Newspaper editors are terrified of angry letters, so once a comic strip gains a foothold with an audience, it tends to stick around for a long time. This is why comic strips are the most conservative entertainment medium. This is why there are still comic strips in the newspaper today that are unchanged from the 1920s and 1930s when they first debuted.

I thought I could use this weakness in the medium to my advantage. I would get these college newspapers hooked on "Jim's Journal," and once they were, I would start charging for it. *The Daily Cardinal* ran "Jim's Journal" for free for about three weeks before they realized people liked it. So, I sent it free to other newspapers until they ran it. And then I waited about a month, and then started charging them. None of them dropped it.

"Jim's Journal" succeeded by being outrageous, both in content and in the way it was sold.

A common side effect of being outrageous is controversy. When you do things differently than the way they've always been done, people sometimes get upset. Fans will be especially devoted and excited—and I got a lot of fan letters—but others will be angry. This kind of controversy gets attention.

At Kansas State University, where the strip ran, students sold "kill Jim" T-shirts. Active campaigns were started on other campuses to pull the comic strip from the newspaper. Readers wrote letters. "It's not funny," they said. "Where's the punchline?" they groused.

"Jim's Journal" defied so many conventions of the four-panel comic-strip format that people were confused and upset. Newspapers wrote stories about the controversy, and they always called me to comment on it. This coverage helped me get the word out about my work.

I didn't think too many of the comic strips in major newspapers were funny. "Garfield," for example, was hokey and unfunny. But would I ever write an angry letter to the editor about it? No. No one would. That's because "Garfield" played the game. Jim Davis, the strip's creator, put punchlines in the last panel. He set up jokes in the panels prior. He told easy-to-get jokes. These were some of the conventions comic strips were expected to follow.

It's when conventions are defied that people get upset. People got upset in Kansas and elsewhere because "Jim's Journal" wasn't playing by the rules. Sometimes the punchline was in the second panel. Sometimes there was no punchline. Sometimes it was just a small relatable moment that petered out.

Years later, engineers at MIT would digitize every "Jim's Journal" cartoon and build an online "create your own 'Jim's Journal' cartoon" game. Mixed-up panels created a random, non-sequitur look at Jim's life. It was fun, not unlike the project that removed the last panel of "Peanuts" to reveal Charles Schulz's pattern of always going down on the penultimate panel, creating a dark and depressing alternate version of Charlie Brown's world.

No one was more surprised than I when *Rolling Stone* magazine listed Jim as one of the nation's college students' top ten favorite writers. I was even more surprised when the book collection of "Jim's Journal" cartoons I had self-published and hand-delivered to bookstores made it onto the *New York Times* bestseller list.

"Jim's Journal's" influence spread further. A college cartoonist named Jeff Kinney, whose strip appeared next to "Jim's Journal" in *The Diamondback* at the University of Maryland, went on to create his own stick-figure comic strip that serves as the journal of the main character—it's a strip that could be confused for "Jim's Journal" given the strikingly similar drawing style. You've heard of it. It's called "Diary of a Wimpy Kid."

A fellow cartoonist at *The Daily Cardinal*, James Sturm, created a brilliantly outrageous cartoon, "The Adventures of Down and Out

Dawg." It was every bit as popular on campus as "Jim's Journal." James was a fun person and knew how to make friends. He was great to me and we respected each other's work. We shared information about how to publish books. James got me involved in my first book of "Jim's Journal" cartoons, a collection of several different artists including a young Chris Ware. The book was called *Commix*. It was self-published and sold in local bookstores. Cartoonist P.S. Mueller, who would later be the voice of *The Onion Radio News* as the character Doyle Redland, wrote the introduction.

James and I swapped comics one day. He drew "Jim's Journal" in the style of "Down And Out Dawg," and I drew "Down And Out Dawg." I made it a "Garfield" parody.

James was fun. He was an extrovert, and a connector, and a good person to know. It was James who first introduced me to the 11x17 sheet of paper that would one day turn into *The Onion*.

5
THE NASCENT ONION

The president of the United States was Ronald Reagan. The big movie at the box office was *Big*, which made Tom Hanks a major box-office star. The "big three" networks, ABC, CBS, and NBC, still ruled TV. George Michael, INXS, and Whitney Houston topped the *Billboard* charts. *USA Today* was seven years old and widely decried as a portent of the "infotainmentization" of journalism. Only about ten percent of households had a personal computer. No one had a cell phone.

In this unrecognizable era, a proto-*Onion* was hatched on a piece of paper, an 11x17 calendar that James Sturm showed me one day on Bloom Street in Madison. It looked like a pancake-house place-mat with ads from local businesses around the edge. It also featured a calendar that listed important dates for students to know (like when classes started). In the center was a big "Down and Out Dawg" cartoon. James told me he'd made a couple hundred dollars doing the project for someone named Tim Keck, who had worked on the ad staff of *The Daily Cardinal*. Tim sold the ads for the calendar.

James introduced me to Tim because Tim was interested in doing a calendar like this with me featuring "Jim's Journal."

A "Jim" calendar never happened. Tim instead partnered with another UW student who, as far as I knew, had no advertising sales experience but was nonetheless a charismatic and capable guy named Chris Johnson.

Tim and Chris were smart, funny, good-looking guys. They were cool. Whenever I saw Chris out and about in town, he always had a different, incredibly beautiful young woman on his arm. But they weren't frat boys or preppies. They weren't schmoozes. They were genuine, intense, and hard-working former nerds, most likely, who had grown into extremely attractive and confident young men.

They invited me to Chris's dorm room one day to tell me about a big new project they were hatching: a college humor magazine called *The Rag.*

I was enchanted by this idea in every respect. First, these two guys were among the most impressive individuals I had ever encountered. Second, the idea of starting a humor magazine filled me with starry-eyed romance. The notion of helping to create something like *Mad* with my own cartoons and comedy stories gave me chills. I was aware of the *Harvard Lampoon* and knew a little about how it spawned *National Lampoon.*

National Lampoon was mostly dead at this point. In recent years it had reduced its publication schedule, lost revenue, and was run by business interests more than creative ones, and—most importantly—it had become embarrassingly unfunny.

Mad, while still thriving, was geared toward younger kids.

So, I thought, maybe this new magazine could fill a niche.

I had no illusions about *The Rag* becoming the next *National Lampoon* or *Mad*, however. These were merely daydreams. Tim and Chris had no money. There was no investor. There was no grand plan. They were just going to start this publication and see if they could make a go of it.

But I didn't care either way. I was excited to be involved in a humor publication of any kind. I liked Tim and Chris. They had some funny ideas. It was a no-brainer.

Tim and Chris wanted me to pull "Jim's Journal" from *The Daily Cardinal* and run it in *The Rag*. I considered it, but thought "Jim's Journal" was much better suited to the *Cardinal*. *The Rag* would be weekly, but "Jim's Journal" worked better as a daily strip. It's to Tim and Chris's credit that they didn't sell me harder. They could have. I would have crumbled under their charms. But they respected my decision. I offered to draw three different comic strips—new comic strips—for *The Rag*, using three distinct drawing styles and three different pseudonyms. I didn't want the magazine to look like a bad high-school yearbook where the one kid who could draw was doing all the comics. I wanted it to look like they had an impressive stable of cartoonists.

I was excited about the possibility of creating new comic strips. I thought I might match or even exceed the success I'd had with "Jim's Journal."

Most people who knew me from "Jim's Journal" didn't know I could draw. The strip was crude. Jim was essentially a stick figure. But this was a stylistic choice. I had gotten to be a good illustrator by this time and had even gotten a few freelance illustrator jobs outside of cartooning.

Meanwhile, Tim and Chris had taken their weekly humor magazine to a printing press and gotten bids on printing the project. The figure was in the thousands of dollars—per issue. Perhaps it was the glossy magazine stock or the full color on the front page, but whatever the case, Tim and Chris had asked the printer to let them know how they could print the publication as cheaply as possible. The answer was that it would have to be printed on newsprint, in black and white.

My heart sank. Who had ever heard of a humor magazine on newsprint? In black and white!? This project was going to be no better than a zine, I thought. I had envisioned something that looked more like *National Lampoon*. But Tim and Chris accepted the reality, as well as the much more affordable printing costs.

The next time I stopped by Chris's dorm room, he and Tim told me they weren't going to call it *The Rag* anymore. The new name was *The Onion*.

This made sense to me. I visited Chris one morning and witnessed him wake up and make breakfast: raw white onion cut up on a piece of untoasted white bread. Tim later said his uncle had seen both him and Chris eating onion sandwiches and suggested the name.

Beyond that excellent inspiration, *The Onion* was simply a good name for a newspaper. It brought to mind the peeling back of layers to get at the facts, like a juicy news story. Looking back, I don't understand why *The Onion* was never in the pantheon of acceptable newspaper names like *The Beacon* or *The Herald*. It's a wonderful name for a newspaper of any kind, especially a legitimate one with real, investigative reporting. But that can't happen now, of course. The name is ruined for all time.

Tim and Chris offered me $20 per cartoon per week for a total of $60 a week. This felt exorbitant to me. They were barely getting paid themselves. Most of the profits from the meager advertisements they were able to sell went toward printing. *The Onion* printed 10,000 copies for its first issue and was only eight pages long, two tabloid sheets, folded.

When I picked up the first issue on August 29, 1988, I wasn't impressed. It had promise, but I didn't think it was anything great. The cover story was a Loch Ness monster parody relocated to Lake Mendota in Madison. The headline was "Lake Mendota Monster Mauls Madison." The cover image was the standard Loch Ness fake photo with Tim sticking his arm out of the water in the shape of a serpent head.

Nonetheless, I believed in Tim and Chris. I had every faith they would get better.

A week later, when the second issue came out, my impression was that they were spreading themselves too thin. It was riddled with typos and generally looked slapped together in a hurry. They were spending all their time working at *The Onion*, they weren't sleeping enough, and they needed some help. So I knocked on their door and essentially volunteered to fill the position of editor. They were delighted to have the help.

They told me later that they had been working on a plan for the third issue: they would take a picture of the two of them mooning the camera, and then run it on the front page with a big banner headline that said, "Fuck You, Readers—We Quit." I don't know if they were joking, but they were certainly overworked and tired.

Tim's naked ass did in fact appear on the cover of issue three, but it was for a different story idea entirely ("Wild Boy of Picnic Point," the report of a boy who lived in a wooded area northwest of campus who was undiscovered by civilization). It seemed Tim was eager, one way or another, to appear naked on the cover of his own newspaper.

For some of the writing, Tim and Chris engaged improv performer Matt Cook to type until the allotted space on certain pages was filled. I was astounded by this process. He was just filling column inches, essentially using improv to write prose.

With no finesse and with an incredibly presumptuous tone, I explained to Matt that articles in newspapers needed structure and editing. One couldn't just type until the column inches were filled, I said.

I later found out Matt was one of the funniest people in Madison. He showed me some videos he'd made that were hilarious. One was a parody of those old mail-order-LP ads on TV where regular people in the grocery store or at picnics mouthed along wholesomely to the songs. His featured hardcore punk songs that had over-the-top swearing and violence in the lyrics. I also found out he'd been part of an improv theater company in Madison called the Arc Improv Theater, where he performed with people like Chris Farley, Joan Cusack, future Conan O'Brien and Stephen Colbert writer Brian Stack, and future *Onion* head writer Todd Hanson.

Matt didn't last long at *The Onion*. I don't know if my horrendous bluster as a new de facto editor pushed him out, if he got bored, or if he just wanted to move on. I had little awareness of how my behavior affected other people, unfortunately. I was focused on only one thing: trying to make *The Onion* funny.

And now, a large part of that responsibility fell on my shoulders. I was coming up with a lot of the stories, brainstorming with Tim, and writing a lot of the jokes. Tim and Chris, however, still came up with a lot of stories on their own.

One of my favorites of theirs was a contest to win a cheese sandwich. They invited readers to write an essay about why America was great, and they would chose the winning essay and present the writer with a free cheese sandwich. Not a grilled-cheese sandwich, but a cold, white-bread, Velveeta Cheese sandwich.

The process for selecting the winner of the cheese-sandwich contest was at best unfair, at worst unethical. The entrants had to submit a picture of themselves with their essay, and pictures were assessed based on how funny the person would look being awarded a cheese sandwich. People who were too good-looking were dismissed outright. A reader who had a nice middle-of-the-road look—an early "area man" prototype—was selected. He also happened to have written the best essay. It was short, wry, and amusing. A nice-looking wood-paneled room at the UW-Madison Rathskeller was staged with a podium and flags to dress it as an appropriate award-ceremony location. Tim and Chris, dressed in suits, handed the winner his cheese sandwich. A photo of the gala event graced the next issue's front page.

Tim and Chris set the early tone of *The Onion*. There was a lot of edgy humor, but also a lot of features that would seem wildly out of place in the current *Onion*, mostly run to provide content of value to student readers, which Tim and Chris felt was important to sell advertising: summaries of the week's soap operas, "The *Onion* Mixer" (a different mixed drink recipe in each issue), "The Genius Puzzle," and "Who's Busted" (an actual reprinting of the UW campus police log of some of the funniest criminal antics of the week).

Tim and Chris understood edgy humor. They liked to push boundaries. This was different from the kind of humor I had been doing. My humor was usually pretty G-rated. I was never too interested in *National Lampoon*. I was into *Mad*. "Jim's Journal" was hyper-innocent, like a mainstream daily comic strip in that way. Stories I had written before I got involved with *The Onion* were practically for kids. Tim and Chris inspired me to expand my repertoire to include more juvenile, shock-value humor, to embrace the endless possibilities of writing not only for humor but also for getting attention.

One of my comic strips in *The Onion* became especially popular. It was the most outrageous one I was drawing. It was "Plebes," a strip that made fun of dumb college guys, a rich target. With "Plebes," I started branching out with more shocking humor of my own, like "Adventures in Party-time Urination," and "Get a Minimum-Wage Job and See How Fast You Can Lose it."

In these first few months, *The Onion* was a lot like *The Stranger*, the alternative weekly in Seattle Tim would later create. More specifically, *The Onion* was an odd mix of *The Stranger*, *Weekly World News*, and the future *Onion*. "Dead Guy Found," the front page story from February 21, 1989, was particularly *Oniony*, as was "Ed Gein—Madman Or Misunderstood Rural Hobbyist?"

I continued to draw my cartoons and occasionally helped out with stories. I stepped away from *The Onion* after I felt I'd helped it get on its feet and get off to a good start. I had coerced my friend Keith from Ellsworth to work for them. He created a comic strip for *The Onion* called "H.J. Frogg's Comic" and wrote a regular column, "Remembering Madison," written in the voice of *The Onion*'s staff psychic, Elicia Caldor, a made-up character (played by Matt Cook in drag) who would go on to write *The Onion*'s horoscopes for many years. The conceit of the column was that it was written in the future, looking back on today.

The Onion seemed to be finding its footing quite nicely in Madison by the spring of 1989. But then Tim and Chris came to me with shocking news.

6
THE WRITERS

After a few months helping out *The Onion* for free, I got a call from Chris letting me know he and Tim weren't going to continue publishing *The Onion*. They were tired and needed to take a break. But instead of ceasing publication, he offered to sell me *The Onion*.

After much discussion, a contract was written up—by a real lawyer. In it, Tim and Chris offered *The Onion* and all its assets for sale to me and two others, *Onion* ad-sales rep Pete Haise and Jonathon Hart Eddy, for one-third ownership each. The plan was that I would oversee editorial, Pete business, and Johnny production (he did all the design and layout for *The Onion* and knew how to use the single Mac lunchbox computer *The Onion* owned). Pete and I would buy out Johnny a year or two later. The sale price was $16,400, to be paid over a few months, out of the paper's revenue. As a down payment, I had to come up with $3,000 cash. It was all the money I had in the world.

Pete and I established a deal early, a gentleman's agreement: he wouldn't tell me what to write, and I wouldn't tell him how to spend the money. Sometimes this deal posed unforeseen problems, like when I was desperate to fund certain priorities that Pete didn't agree with, or when Pete and his ad staff would work for months to convince a national advertiser to run a full-page ad, not realizing I was planning a front page story making fun of the same advertiser. Problems aside, it was a fair arrangement that gave *Onion* editorial far more power than editorial has in other publications. At virtually all other magazines or entertainment outlets, the lawyers and the shareholders have the final say on editorial matters. Even *The Onion* does it this way now.

Jay Rath was a local cartoonist who palled around with James Sturm and me. He had a comic strip in *Isthmus*, Madison's alternative weekly newspaper, about a cow named Bossie. It was actually an ad for a local grocery store but he produced it as a comic strip. Jay told me I would be making a mistake to buy *The Onion*. He thought it would be wiser to start my own publication. I knew how much work the first year of *The Onion* had been, so I rejected his idea. I was already putting so much of my soul into *The Onion*, the decision to buy it was easy. I urged Jay to go in on it with me, but he wasn't interested.

Tim and Chris were *The Onion*'s first writers. Matt Cook came next. There was another writer named Mark Pitsch who wrote a regular column for Tim and Chris called "Catch the Pig" about silly and random subjects of local interest. Two young soap-opera-obsessed women, Sandra Schlies and Susan Rathke, wrote *The Onion*'s soap-opera summaries starting in the first issue and continuing for years after. It was one of the paper's most popular features.

After I became co-owner and editor-in-chief of *The Onion*, as of the summer of 1989, I inherited the soap-opera experts and Tim Keck. I wrote pretty much everything else. Matt Cook was gone by then. Pete occasionally wrote a sports-betting column because it was something he knew about. He took on the fake name Vince "The Bull" Meecham, and we pictured him as an old sporto character who looked like Jimmy the Greek. I thought the subject matter was suitably arcane and ridiculous. The fact that Pete knew anything about sports betting at all was funny to me, as well as the idea that a newspaper would run a column about it.

I engaged my brother Alan to write a column about how to tan animal hides, something he had taught himself to do while living outside and in an unheated horse barn for a winter in Wisconsin. He himself looked like a mountain man and wore only clothes that he made himself out of hides he tanned, often from roadkill he found and cleaned.

Alan's character was one of the first in a pattern of "runners": series-type stories *The Onion* would do in the early years that were comprised of several stories or features and would culminate in a punchline. "Grizzly Al," as we called him, wrote a few columns, and then the columns abruptly ended. They had all been a set up for the news-story punchline: "Missing Students' Corpses Found In Hide Tanner's Basement."

My brother also provided the art for one of my comic strips, "Professor Hornby's Figures in History." He could draw in that "Mark Trail" style better than I could. He also drew a realistic flaccid penis that ran big on *The Onion*'s front page on September 19, 1989, with the screaming headline, "Our Society Is In The Grip Of Penis Fear."

The "Penis Fear" issue was an attention-grabber. People were starting to talk about *The Onion*.

Stories I wrote included "Scientists Baffled By Amazing Worm Boy," the boy raised by worms in the wild who therefore took on worm characteristics, and "It's a Convoy!" a 70s throwback piece that pretended all the kids of the day were into CB-radio lingo and driving big rigs.

CB lingo and my brother's detailed and accurate hide-tanning instructions were the kinds of unrelatable subjects I liked for *The Onion*. The ironic effect of offering college-age readers how-to columns about wildly irrelevant and confounding information was amusing to me.

These kinds of articles were the first hint of satire in *The Onion*. The subtext was that media is tone deaf to the needs of its consumers. This dichotomy set *The Onion* apart from other college publications, which routinely printed pandering articles like "How to make the most of your study time."

In truth, in *The Onion*'s first year, it did in fact run a column produced by the UW–Madison Writing Lab. It featured real, practical writing advice like "Some Plain Talk About Writing Essay Exams" and "Tips for Academic Success." I wanted to mock Tim and Chris's earnest attempt to make *The Onion* useful.

In *The Onion*'s second year, we heightened the irony and made function follow form with stories like "Pen Stolen from Dorm Study Area" on the front page with World War III-sized type. We mixed in madcap with stories like "Food Fights Mar This Year's Macaroni & Cheese Bakeoff." And we started experimenting with analogy with stories like "VapoRub: The Silent Killer."

Despite Tim and Chris selling *The Onion*, Tim remained involved. He and I spent a lot of time coming up with funny concepts. He was a delightful brainstormer, and would visit me at the radio station when I worked the late shifts or weekend shifts. My job entailed hitting the play button on a tape recorder once per hour. The rest of my time was free. So, we sat around on the top floor of Vilas Hall in the slick lobby of Wisconsin Public Radio and Television and laughed ourselves silly coming up with ridiculous *Onion* headlines. Vilas Hall was an enormous concrete structure that had been built after the 1960s anti-war protests on campus. One of the stated benefits of the building was that its M.C. Escher-like design made it impossible for students to storm or block entrances. One of the stories Tim and I concocted was "Drunken Carousers Overturn Vilas Hall." When the story ran, it featured one of *The Onion*'s first Photoshop-altered images, a ridiculous picture of Vilas Hall tipped on its end.

Photoshop was a new software tool that *The Onion*'s computer barely had the RAM necessary to operate. The earlier versions of the program had no layers, so altering photos was a painstaking process of cutting part of one image, pasting it on top of another image, and then holding down the "option" key while erasing all the parts around the pasted image needed to make it look photoreal.

Beyond this ragtag group of writers held over from *The Onion*'s first year, I didn't recruit many writers, at least not at first. *Onion* writers found me.

Rich Dahm came by the office one day. He seemed like a nice, smart guy. I asked him to write a story, and in a day or two he produced a submission that was well written and funny. Pretty soon he was writing and hanging out in the office regularly.

Rich worked as a school-bus driver during the day. Now he was working at *The Onion* all night, just like me. He started writing a regular column called "Rich's kids," inspired by his relationship with the elementary-school kids he drove on the bus. The column featured mostly made-up stories of Rich and a gang of imaginary kids getting into mischief or learning valuable lessons about life, like in a bad *ABC Afterschool Special*. He also produced the regular feature: "The Cultural Idiocy Quiz," which glorified useless pop-culture knowledge (of which Rich was a master). It was a response to the E. D. Hirsch bestseller, *Cultural Literacy*, which had taken the nation by storm in the late 1980s by revealing how uneducated most of the population was.

Rich and I would often stay up all night, drink cokes, eat pizzas, and crack each other up. One night, the two of us brainstormed enough headlines to fill *The Onion*'s docket for the next few months: headlines like "Hail To The King! A Jubilant Nation Cheers As U.S. Converts To Monarchy," "*The Onion* Acquires New Envelope Moistener," "Emperor of Saturn To Enslave Us All," and more runners.

We hatched a multi-part series featuring the character of the "belt-sanding hoodlum," a criminal who maimed several people with a belt-sander. In the stories we planned, he was always celebrated for his good deeds, as if he had the best publicist in the world, or *The Onion* was somehow complicit in trying to reshape his public image. Headlines announced, "Belt-Sanding Hoodlum Rescues Drowning Child," and "Belt-Sanding Hoodlum Receives 'Outstanding Citizen' Award." Years later, "Belt-Sanding Hoodlum Announces Bid For U.S. Presidency."

The belt-sanding hoodlum was played by Todd Hanson.

Another storyline Rich and I devised was one involving Lucky the Chimp. He was a plain-looking clip-art chimpanzee illustration we'd found. He was billed as *The Onion*'s mascot.

Lucky the Chimp would appear in what we called "deadheads" (empty spaces in the newspaper that were not filled by ads, so had to be populated with filler that we tried to turn into jokes, fake ads, public-service announcements, or in-house ads for *The Onion*). Lucky the Chimp was featured in deadheads for a few months, steadily increasing in their frequency, suggesting he was becoming a beloved part of *The Onion*'s brand. He had his own catch phrase ("I'm goin' bananas!") and his own theme song:

> *Lucky, Lucky, Lucky the Chimp*
> *We love you*
> *Lucky, Lucky, Lucky the Chimp*
> *Catch those crooks!*

The Lucky the Chimp storyline culminated in an issue of *The Onion* saturated by Lucky the Chimp appearances, as if *The Onion* was ramming this brand mascot down readers' throats hard. In the very next issue, however, we ran only a single eighth-page deadhead announcing, "Lucky the Chimp, *The Onion*'s mascot, is for sale."

He never appeared in *The Onion* again, making people wonder (we hoped) what horror the animal might have visited upon *The Onion* to warrant such a cold dismissal.

Another writer who came into the office to finagle himself an unpaid job writing for *The Onion* was Shaun Mulheron. Shaun dabbled in ad sales and was an edgy kind of guy. He drank heavily, had a pleasantly aggressive personality, and smirked constantly. He once brought his two-year-old niece to the office. She crawled around on the desks. We took her picture and I put it on the front page with the headline, "Whose Baby Is This?"

Todd Hanson was someone both Rich and I knew. Before he

dropped out of college, Todd had lived in the same dorm as Rich. I had seen Todd at *The Daily Cardinal*. I had also seen him working at Capital Center Foods. He would joke around with customers in a friendly way but at the same time subversively mocking them. He was handsome, with a rich, senatorial voice, and he was incredibly smart. He dressed like Judd Nelson in *The Breakfast Club* and always appeared unkempt (which made him the perfect belt-sanding hoodlum). Todd was someone you couldn't miss.

He began contributing jokes to some of *The Onion*'s regular features like the Snapshot (a parody of the *USA Today* Snapshot) and "What Do *You* Think?" (still a feature in *The Onion*, though now called "American Voices"), which presented the opinions of random people on the street to the news of the day, the joke being that they were the same people every week.

Despite his biting sense of humor, Todd was one of the warmest and most emotionally expressive people I'd ever met. Everyone who knew Todd knew he struggled with depression and often had trouble holding his life together. He was terrible with deadlines and for years didn't open his mail. It seemed to me his mind was simply too intellectually curious about himself and the world around him that he couldn't be bothered with mundane worldly concerns like paying rent, holding down a job, or staying in school. In later years, he would appear in stories he wrote that were personal tales of his own struggles told in AP-style newswriting: "Area Man Makes It Through Day," "Utter Failure To Spend Rest of Day in Bed," and others.

John Krewson came from a liquor store on State Street called Badger Liquor. He was a solidly built, fast-talking genius who suffered from migraines and almost never turned in a story on time.

The Onion recruited a number of good writers from Badger Liquor. They were known for posting unnecessarily clever, hand-made signs in the window promoting drinking. One of them was Joe Garden. Joe was a burlesque performer and nudist, a wiry, lively guy with pollywog arms and legs that always seemed to be moving. Joe created a pathetic motorhead teen columnist for *The Onion* named Jim Anchower.

The Onion had a nude man we could call on whenever we needed one for a photo: Don Traeger, my brother Alan's landlord. He was older, heavyset, and looked really funny naked. He worked as a referee in his day job but enjoyed appearing naked in *The Onion*. He was first featured in the story "Would-Be Superhero Can Only Fly When Naked." Several others would follow.

But if Don wasn't available, Joe was happy to step in. He was a good replacement, especially as he began to age and develop a gut.

Maria Schneider was a little old lady who just happened to be in her 20s like the rest of us. She was as sweet and soft-spoken as a kindly elderly aunt. She loved her cats and paid her rent on time. But when you needed gangsta slang or swearing, it would spew forth from her spectacularly. She created the character of Herbert Kornfeld for *The Onion*, the accountant who played out gangsta fantasies in his mind. She also wrote the sad and hilarious Jean Teasdale columns.

Like the other writers and me, Maria had struggles. She harnessed her troubled childhood in her comic strip, "Pathetic Geek Stories," tales sent in by readers of their most humiliating memories from childhood. Maria would illustrate them.

Dan Vebber was a cartoonist who kept sending cartoons to *The Onion*. Rich and I didn't like his cartoons, but he was so persistent that he finally became a writer. Dan was a very binary character. Things were either the greatest ever or the worst ever. There was no in-between with Dan. He worked hard and was a natural leader. In a few short years he became an editor.

A shocking number of *Onion* writers had been cartoonists at *The Daily Cardinal* but many of them came to *The Onion* independently of each other. Another was Mike Loew, a lanky redhead whose attention to detail quickly made him *The Onion*'s first graphics editor. At what passed for his job interview, he told me he used to paint those little green plastic soldiers as a kid. He explained that he painted not only the whites of their eyes but also the iris, the pupil, and even a tiny dot of white inside the pupil to suggest a reflection of light. I hired him on the spot.

Kelly Ambrose was a drunken college student who was one of the funniest people I've ever met. He wasn't just funny on paper; his life was like a comedic performance art piece. Kelly created his own greeting card company. It was a pathetic effort, which was part of its charm. He wrote the cards in ballpoint pen on lined notebook paper that he folded himself. Sometimes the fringes were still on the edge of the paper. He partnered with another *Onion* writer, Andy Selsberg, and christened the project Kel-Dee cards.

They didn't sell more than a handful of cards, but they were the funniest cards I'd ever seen, far better than the corporate committee-written greeting cards available at gift stores. One card said "Happy birthday" on the front. On the inside it said "From me and Dean." Below the copy Kelly had taped a driver's license he'd found formerly belonging to some guy named Dean.

As more writers came to *The Onion*, the more I saw they were of a kind. They were the misfits and the nerds, the outcasts and the dropouts. They were like me. They'd had unpleasant childhoods and turned to comedy as a way to cope. *The Onion* was their refuge.

I loved all these writers. They were smart, funny, and authentic. Being around them made me feel like a better person. *The Onion* writer's room felt like a dorm lounge or a family rec room with a lot of mischievous but caring siblings.

I began to realize it was people with problems—people who didn't fit in anywhere else—who were the best *Onion* writers. And with *The Onion*, I wanted to create a protective cocoon for them, a place where they could have fun and be funny and be free of worry from the indignities of corporate life or minimum wage jobs, where by-the-book supervisors would fire them for not showing up, performance-focused bosses would chide them for being slow or weak, and peers would blast them for making mistakes.

Writers at *The Onion* could disappear for days on end, suffer an emotional breakdown and "ghost" me, failing to respond to my repeated phone calls. Kelly would go on long drinking binges. But I would never fire them or reprimand them for such behavior. They always had a home at *The Onion*.

Maria once disappeared for nearly a week. When she returned, she told me, "I had to give my cat medicine." It was all I needed to hear. I welcomed her back to the writer's room, no questions asked.

One writer, Tim Harrod, originally contacted me by email in the mid 90s. His subject heading was "Area Loser Wants Job." I invited him to submit headlines. He did, and they were good. So, I called him. I found out he was nearly 30 years old and living in his mother's basement, professing to have been too insecure to leave the house for several years. I thought, "Just the kind of talent we're looking for!"

7
A MERITOCRACY

In the movie *Die Hard 2*, a band of U.S. Soldiers-turned-terrorists takes over the Dulles Airport in Washington. Bruce Willis tries unsuccessfully to convince the airport police that these aren't just common luggage thieves. An Army Special Forces team is called in to dispatch the terrorists. After a firefight between the Special Forces and the terrorists, Willis discovers that the Army team is using blanks—they're in league with the terrorists! To convince the slow-witted captain of the airport police what's happened, Willis barges into the headquarters with one of the machine guns he stole off a thug he offed. He fires it right there in the office, directly at the captain. The captain is shaken but unharmed, proving to everyone assembled that the cartridges are indeed blanks, and there's a larger conspiracy afoot!

There's a larger conspiracy, alright, but it has nothing to do with soldiers and terrorists. It involves the movie industry's poetic license when it comes to blanks, and it has deadly consequences; it's one of the most dangerous fictions in movies.

When characters in action movies use blanks in their guns, they can walk up to another character in the movie and shoot them in the head and no one gets hurt, because the unspoken rule in movies is that blanks are harmless. The truth is, blanks are deadly.

A good firearms handler on a TV or movie set takes great care to explain to everyone in the cast and crew how careful they need to be with "blank" weapons, to never point a gun loaded with blanks at anyone, and to never fire it unless the stunt team has coordinated all the blocking. The firing of the gun is done at an angle or with a telephoto lens to make the victim appear close to the gun. Stunt doubles with body armor are used if need be. Even from 20 feet away a blank cartridge can cause serious damage.

But the myth persists. Several actors and movie crew members have been seriously injured—even killed—by blanks over the years. Could this be because the myth portrayed by movie blanks has seeped into the popular consciousness, and we all just go through life blissfully accepting the idea that "blanks" means "safe"?

Probably.

There's another myth just as backwards as the blanks myth. Though to my knowledge no one has died as a result of it, thank goodness. The only consequence is a lot of bad jokes. The myth is how the comedy writers' room works.

In the writers' rooms of movies and TV shows, a talented writer barges in excitedly and says, "I came up with a great idea!" The others ask what it is, the writer tells them, and they all laugh. "The joke is perfect! That's the joke that will open tonight's show!" Or here's another common scenario: a young writer types something up—a first draft with no revisions—and rips it out of the typewriter (so many writers in movies still use typewriters) and shows it to his boss. His boss reads it, laughs, and says, "This is genius!"

It pains me to think of all the bad material and all the bad jokes that have come out of meetings modeled after this inaccurate movie cliché. (Not as much as it pains me that people got shot by blanks, but we all must pick our battles. I care about good jokes.)

The truth is that a real writers' room is nothing like either of these scenarios. Writers of comedy in real life work hard, churning out hundreds of jokes at their desks, often in abject solitude. When they reach a critical mass, they show their boss lists of jokes or long drafts of copy. This boss will invariably shrug and say, "Well, joke number thirty-eight is okay," or "You're getting close to it in this paragraph, but these others don't work." Always, the message is, "You need to rework it."

The *Onion* writers' room is, historically, even more gloomy. Sometimes other writers' rooms do in fact involve funny people pitching ideas. They sometimes even involve those ideas being well received. But this is the exception rather than the rule. In the *Onion* writers' room, writers don't pitch their own jokes. And the identity of the writer of each joke is kept hidden. Writers almost never stand up upon hearing a pitch to say "That's genius!" Writers are invited to respond honestly and critically to every idea.

None of us had any idea how to structure a writers' room when *The Onion* began. The only "writers' rooms" I'd been in were those of my friends making cassette radio plays or writing scripts. But I knew from those meetings that the natural process—the process people fall into if left to their own judgment—is flawed. It leads to bad jokes. The alpha in the group gets his (it's almost always a his) ideas approved more because he's louder and more outgoing. The more likable people in the group get more ideas accepted because they're more likable. None of this has anything to do with the inherent quality of the jokes. As humans, we're blind to our own biases. We can't take ourselves out of the situation. When we hear a funny idea, we can't detach our feelings for the creator from the funny idea. The same goes for bad ideas.

Making the *Onion* writers' room an honest place was a challenge. It's difficult to tell people their ideas aren't good, but it's essential for quality. Maintaining morale can be a struggle, but there are a few ways around it.

For starters, I made writers come to meetings with 15 or 20 ideas instead of one. If someone pitches one idea, you have the unpleasant task of telling them to their face, "Your one idea is no good." Nobody wants that. If they submit 15 or 20, it's now socially acceptable to say "number four was pretty good," putting a positive spin on the sad fact that you just rejected 95 percent of their ideas.

Removing the writer from the pitch entirely was an important innovation at *The Onion*. Instead of pitching stories or concepts that might take some explaining, we would pitch the headline only. After all, what else is needed? Readers wouldn't get a prolonged pitch about how interesting or funny this article was. All they would see at first is the headline. And that headline had better (1) communicate the idea clearly, simply and briefly, and (2) be funny enough to make them want to read the article. Therefore, *Onion* headlines would be judged by the same standard.

The way I liked to do it was to have one person in the meeting—the person with the least interesting voice—read all the headlines from all the writers. By reading them in a monotone, giving them no life or "sell," this would replicate the reader's experience. The reader would get no razzmatazz or pitch or sell when they saw the headline in black-and-white. How could we expect to judge material impartially if we were ginning it up and making it grander than it really was?

Another important practice at *The Onion* is volume. I knew from my own experience that over 95 percent of anyone's ideas are garbage. In order to get the best ideas out of anyone, that person had to generate a lot of ideas. All writers brought 15 or 20 ideas. In total, sometimes hundreds of ideas would be read at every *Onion* writers' meeting. At the end of the meeting, only a handful of jokes would be moved to the short list where they might still be cut later by an editor. But only when more than half of the writers in attendance approve an idea does it advance to that stage.

One of the nicest compliments *The Onion* receives is that it's consistent. Most comedy shows or publications have some good episodes or issues and some bad episodes or issues, but people told us *The Onion* had something funny in every issue. *Esquire* gave us high praise indeed when they wrote that *The Onion* was "the most consistently hilarious spot on the flogged dead horse of American comedy." We often received fan letters telling us essentially the same thing.

Were the writers at *The Onion* any smarter or better than writers at other comedy publications or TV shows? Of course not. There are smart, funny writers everywhere. But *Onion* writers worked within a tight system, a meritocracy that served as a sieve where volumes of jokes were reviewed dispassionately until only the funniest remained. In this way, true gems were discovered.

These two counterintuitive and myth-busting strategies, (1) focusing on quantity to achieve quality and (2) judging material on its merits, apart from ego, cause the best work to rise to the top. Only by producing the best ideas can you ever hope to succeed in the Attention Economy or the Love Economy.

8
NO NAMES, NO CREDIT

Before *The Onion*, humor writing always had the writer's name on it. The humor authors and novelists of the early 20th century like Thurber and Benchley were known to their readers. Mark Twain was the most famous person in the world. This standard practice extended to group efforts like magazines. At both *Mad* and *National Lampoon*, writers were made into mini-celebrities whose names were on everything they wrote and who were often pictured and talked about in "foto funnies" in the *Lampoon* and letters in *Mad*.

Why?

Well, it's fair. People should get credit for their work. But is it in the best interest of a brand like a magazine?

The custom hurt the *Lampoon*. With writers putting their names on stories and becoming celebrities, fans associated them with the magazine. When well-known writers inevitably moved on to work in Hollywood or on *SNL*, readers knew it and didn't like it. They would say, "The *Lampoon* isn't funny now that Doug Kenney left," or "The *Lampoon* is nothing without Henry Beard."

I watched in fascination as *National Lampoon*'s esteem as a brand plummeted through the 1980s. By 1990 is was a withered husk of its former self, sticking its name on every crappy juvenile shock-value teen movie it could find. It seemed to be trying hard to destroy its own good name.

The same thing happened with *Spy*. Graydon Carter and Kurt Andersen were the founders, owners, and primary creative force behind the sharp writing and biting satirical edge that made the magazine great. When they sold *Spy* in 1991 and stopped writing for it, the noticeable drop in quality corresponded to the disappearance of their names from the masthead. Readers like me knew they were gone and immediately lost faith in the publication.

I didn't want the same thing to happen to *The Onion*.

Tim and Chris were very much descendent of Kenney, Beard, Carter and Andersen. They were articulate, camera-ready, funny, and made excellent celebrity writers of their own humor newspaper. They put themselves on the cover of issue five (the cheese-sandwich winner) playing themselves, laying the rails for just such a celebrity-publisher track.

After I started to help edit and *The Onion*'s voice continued to evolve, this kind of behavior morphed into something different. I appeared on the cover of issue four (a look back at the history of the paper with the headline, "*The Onion*'s Early Years"). Matt Cook appeared in many issues. But we were masked, he as *The Onion*'s staff psychic (as well as an anonymous sperm donor), me as *Onion* founder T. Herman Zweibel. This began a long trend of *Onion* writers and other staff appearing in photos in *The Onion* playing fictional characters. Todd appeared frequently, as did Joe, Maria, and just about everyone else. Chris Karwowski was a writer who was pictured frequently. In contrast to his extraordinary comic mind, Chris looked like a nondescript middle-aged Midwestern dullard with his round face, thinning hair, and glasses—the ideal "area man." He appeared dozens of times as local men, schlubs, and as a model for "Heterosexual Men's Fashion." He donned a sexy silk shirt and struck a dreamy album-cover pose as "The Polish Salina" on the cover of *The Onion*

Magazine, perhaps his finest hour.

Only Rich appeared in face and name repeatedly in *The Onion* with a cartoon caricature of him and a byline for his column, "Rich's Kids." But he was the exception.

On the whole, no one knew our names. In the *Onion* masthead, names were listed but no one knew our job titles. We used nonsensical joke titles for years. One week it would be Spinal Tap song titles, another week it would be characters from *Hee Haw*. Furthermore, we jumbled the names from time to time; sometimes I was at the top, sometimes Pete, sometimes the delivery driver. Readers didn't know who was in charge or who did what. I liked it that way. I wanted to keep things a mystery.

Beyond merely listing silly job titles, we actually didn't have real job titles. Pete was responsible for selling the ads and paying the bills. I was responsible for filling the pages. There was no "editor" or "publisher" or "CEO." The company had no org chart. Some people were writers and they worked mostly with me, though occasionally they helped Pete write ad copy. Designers laid out the paper and also designed the ads. It was an unstructured, catch-as-catch-can group, but everyone knew what the goal was: to produce the funniest publication we could. It was no more complicated than that.

Job titles started to appear on commissioned ad-salespeople's business cards at first, because they needed to look professional out in the world. After a few years, designer Jun Ueno made nice-looking business cards for writers and editors. I never used mine, so eventually asked him to stop making them.

The tipping point was when *Onion* ad-sales rep Michael Hirsch, who would later produce both of my feature films, wrote a four-part series of investigative articles for *The Onion* in the early 90s inspired by his time in Europe when he studied abroad. They were funny breakfast-related articles. One was "The International House of Pancakes: Is It Truly International?" Another was "The Myth of the Continental Breakfast."

Michael wanted to clip the articles and put them in his portfolio for future writing jobs. So, he and I negotiated an exception to our no-names policy for these stories. I agreed to put his real name on the pieces.

But Michael seemed untrusting. Before the first article ran, he asked me, "My name will go on the articles, right?"

I assured him it would. But he kept asking. He even came in the paste-up room on the weekend when Rich and I were working against the clock to get everything done by the Sunday night deadline.

"You sure my name is gonna end up on the column?"

"That's right, Mike," I said, clipped. "Now please get lost. Let us work."

After that, I conspired with Rich to spell Michael's name wrong on the piece, changing the byline from "Michael Hirsch" to "Hal Hirsch." The whole series was bylined this way.

He thought it was funny, and I continued to call him Hal for years after.

Hal Mirsch was the beginning of the end of the culture of *Onion* writers putting their names on stories.

The incident indirectly led to a recurring joke at *The Onion* that I enjoyed, which was purposefully getting people's names wrong. I delighted in misspelling Bill Clinton's name especially. A headshot of Clinton for a story about the war in Bosnia or some other heavy subject would be captioned simply, "President Bill Climpton." We upped the ante when we named "Bill Climpton" *The Onion*'s Man of the Year in 1996 as part of a big front-page feature. The funniest part for me was receiving carefully hand-written letters from concerned readers alerting us to the error.

The brand we were building at *The Onion* was one of a faceless news organization; an established, powerful beacon of truth that handed the news down from on high and openly dismissed its readers as dopes, dummies, and layabouts. "You are dumb," was *The Onion*'s official slogan for a long time. In Latin, on our masthead, it was "Tu stultus es." To live out the most heightened manifestation of that brand—to be the most outrageous version of ourselves that we could—we hid staff names and made it a truly faceless organization. The more impersonal and cold the voice of *The Onion*, the more it would live up to that vision.

I wanted *The Onion* to survive any staff change. I wanted *The Onion* itself to be the celebrity, the voice that people knew and recognized. The effort would take many years of chiseling, through trial and error, experimenting with various types of newspaper comedy (parodying *Weekly World News*, pandering to readers, making *The Onion* useful, and making *The Onion* fun), but when we found that serious news voice, the strict AP style that *The Onion* is known for today, I knew we had found the right voice. It was the funniest, the most satirical, and in perfect alignment with the character archetype *The Onion* was channeling: the bumbling authority. By spouting nonsense in a serious tone, every word of *The Onion* would drip with irony. That was our brand.

Over time, that voice and that tone became so identified with *The Onion,* and not with any one writer, that writers could come and go and it didn't matter. The quality would sometimes slip, but we always had the luxury of secrecy and could easily recover, find our footing, and project the image of a consistent brand.

Another reason this unusual practice made sense for *The Onion* is that stories weren't usually written by one person. The headline would be thought up by one writer, and the first draft of the story would be assigned to someone else. The draft would usually come in in rough shape and the editor would have to rewrite it. In a week when things ran smoothly, the entire staff of writers would have a chance to read the editor's version and make notes or suggest changes. Sometimes whole paragraphs from other writers would be inserted into a piece. It was like writing by committee.

Still another rationale for eliminating writers' names from stories is that it mimics the reader's experience. I always had the feeling writers at the *Lampoon* were playing to the camera for their own benefit whenever they would make themselves part of the comedy. It wasn't funny. Readers just want to laugh; they don't want to see desperate writers waving to their moms during a fleeing moment in the spotlight.

In the late 80s, this notion was grand hubris. *Mad* was an institution. *National Lampoon* had been a cultural phenomenon. *Spy* was the bright spot on American satire. *The Onion*, by contrast, was a small college humor newspaper. Every month when the new *Spy* came out, I salivated over it and felt embarrassed. They were a full-color glossy magazine distributed nationally, featuring the best writing in the world. I looked at *The Onion*, printed on concrete-gray newsprint, and could only shake my head. (Granted, sometimes we sprung for the "good" newsprint, which was heavier, and a little closer to a light beige.) *The Onion* was pathetic by comparison; I knew it would never be as good as *Spy*.

In time *The Onion* became known for its odd decision to hide the names of its writers on stories. Media coverage, which started happening to us around the mid to late 90s, posed another challenge. How would we keep *The Onion* faceless yet still take advantage of opportunities to promote it?

Todd was the face I preferred to put out front to do interviews. He was great on camera—funny, insightful, concise, and likable. But when *The Onion* got more well-known, I tried to mix it up. I put myself out there along with different writers here and there—and occasionally Pete—so that no one person would become identified too singularly with *The Onion*.

Had I been interested in my own fame instead of *The Onion*'s, I could have written a column and put it on the front page every week, like Stan Lee did with Marvel. I could have had my own catch phrase like "Excelsior!" I could have re-named the publication *Scott Dikkers' The Onion*. This would have been great for me, in terms of building my personal platform, but it would have set up *The Onion* for a disaster on the scale of the *Lampoon's* fall from grace.

Since I was the editor-in-chief and co-owner, I knew it would be natural for people to tag me as the "lone genius" responsible for it all and turn me into some kind of celebrity writer. It was therefore important to me to preemptively take credit away from myself. I knew such credit would hurt the brand. So, I always credited the team. I learned early that credit is cheap. When I can credit someone who works with me on a shared accomplishment and take myself out of it, it costs me nothing but makes them feel great. It's an excellent way to energize the people who work for you.

The writers of Sid Caesar's *Your Show of Shows* did this kind of magnanimous credit sharing. Whenever a writer would talk about another writer, they would say, "First of all, I have to tell you that Carl Reiner is a genius," "Imogene Coca was a first-rate genius," and "Neil Simon was an absolute genius." They did this without fail. I once told the *Onion* writers that I wanted us to pledge to talk the same way about each other in the future if we're ever interviewed for a documentary about *The Onion*. They're a cynical bunch, so this was a lot to ask. But sometimes I catch them doing it, which always makes me happy.

I wanted to build a brand that was stronger than *National Lampoon* and *Spy*, one that would survive ups and downs and staff changes. If I ever left (which I would do several times), I didn't want readers to know or suspect that there was a change in the quality. If there were ever major staff shakeups (and there would be), I wanted the name *The Onion* to remain a consistent fixture, with any particular staff change going unnoticed.

A great schism would strike *The Onion* in the early 10s, and this odd no-names practice would be put to the test. Could it preserve *The Onion's* unique comic voice in the face of certain doom?

9
KEEPING THINGS WEIRD

Business consultants nowadays tell us there's a "creative class," highly imaginative people who aren't interested in being boxed in by traditional, institutional organizations. These people think differently, dress differently, look strange, and sometimes don't shower. They would rather drop out, live in poverty, and practice with their band than try to fit in in some stifling office environment.

A lot of corporate managers don't know how to recruit, work with, or motivate people in the creative class. They're more comfortable with "normal" people who work in cubicles 9-to-5.

For these creatives, buttoned-up corporate culture is not only unappealing, it's part of a larger problem. It's just another way society is trying to constrain them. Corporate life is a prime target of their mockery and contempt.

An op-ed headline from *The Onion* on February 3, 1998, summed up my feelings on the issue: "I Just Love Corporations!"

If the irony of that headline isn't obvious to you, you're probably one of the "normals."

Corporations move like sloths. Every decision has to be made by a board or committee. Any bold or groundbreaking action is met with skepticism, fear, or outright rejection.

"You'd better be there at 9 a.m. or there'll be hell to pay."

"Those jeans might be appropriate for Casual Friday, but on a Wednesday?!"

"Ooh, management is never going to go for that idea."

For creative people this kind of stifling existence is bullshit. Why can't work be more like play? To succeed with Outrageous Marketing, you need creative minds to imagine just how outrageous things can be. And these people need to be free to create. They need to feel welcome and appreciated. Their penchant for being different, flaunting convention, and maybe breaking some rules, has to be embraced.

Onion writers broke a lot of rules.

By the fall of 1989, we had moved out of Tim and Chris's flat on East Johnson to a small basement office on West Gilman, just off State Street. There were no office hours outside of the weekly writers' meeting. Writers came in whenever they wanted. Sometimes they didn't come in at all. We worked all night sometimes, even pulling "all-weekenders" (a variant of the all-nighter entailing no sleep from Friday night to Monday morning). Writers slept in the office, screamed at each other in the office, and sometimes had complete emotional breakdowns in the office.

They were, however, relentlessly creative.

To wit, in the mid 90s a UW-Madison undergrad had gone missing under mysterious circumstances. Fliers were posted all over campus with her picture and the headline, "Have You Seen This Woman?" followed by details for contacting authorities. One day I saw a similar flier around town. It said "Have You Seen This Man?" and it was a picture of the original actor who played Al on *Happy Days*. It was a wildly inappropriate and edgy parody. I loved it.

I found out it came from a local woman named Carol Kolb.

Another bit of street theater Carol maintained was the Madison Museum of Bathroom Tissue. She collected toilet paper from restrooms whenever she went somewhere notable on vacation, like

Graceland or Mount Rushmore. She would label where each roll came from and display it in her apartment. She got the museum listed in official museum registries and gave tours to people who came to visit. Soon others heard about the museum and began sending her toilet paper they collected when they went on vacation. In time almost all the walls of her apartment were covered floor-to-ceiling with toilet paper from all over the world. She had toilet paper from the Louvre, the Great Wall of China, and even the White House. The White House toilet paper was presented in a special glass display case.

Another great stunt Carol perpetrated was digging a hole in the grassy median in front of her apartment. It was about a foot wide and a couple of feet deep. Next to it she put a small placard with a desperate-looking hand-written note that said, "Who took our baby?" The sign explained further that their newborn had died, that they buried it here in the grassy median, and some monster had dug up the body.

I hired Carol as soon as I could.

When she joined the staff, the *Onion* office was an unusual place. It was like a dorm hangout lounge with beanbag chairs and wacky signs and writing all over the walls. All the former Badger Liquor employees put up signs wherever they worked, we learned.

There was a fair amount of nudity around the office. Sometimes it was nudity in the publication, which was expected. One of *The Onion*'s ad reps, Chris Knight, was a professional stripper who appeared on the front page in his G-string. Staffers posed in a group photo for the front-page story, "UW Cuts Funding of Coed Naked Sports." I myself posed half-naked to play a porn star. Even my partner Pete was featured shirtless in a parody of a phone-sex ad that urged advertisers to call *The Onion*: "Pete is hot and ready to talk advertising with you *now!*"

Other times the nudity wasn't related to the publication. I once picked up Todd for work and he paraded around his efficiency apartment naked. Kelly had a fun trick he would do in the office where he would show you one testicle. *Wired* did a big story about *The Onion* in the late 90s. On the day the photographer came to take a picture of the writers' room in action, Tim Harrod offered to take off all his clothes for a funny shot that would show the staff in a meeting together with Tim standing among them, the only one bare-ass naked.

Some of this behavior might seem disturbing. At the time it was merely a side effect of hiring weirdos and being a company run by weirdos. It was never inappropriate. The point was to get perilously close to inappropriate and have fun doing it. Appropriate humor, after all, isn't particularly funny. Satire needs a sense of danger.

Sometimes things were just a little strange. Robert Siegel was a New York native who had come to Madison with the express purpose of getting a job at the big comedy institution in town: the Wisconsin Public Radio show *Whad'Ya Know?* with Michael Feldman. To our great benefit, Robert ended up at *The Onion* instead. He was an incredible writer, but he was strange. He was a recluse like me, it seemed, and didn't socialize much with the other writers. He also claimed to have never eaten a fruit or vegetable. By way of explaining himself, he tried to describe how disturbing the thin skin on a grape was to him. I often hounded him to try a grape, a cherry, or an orange, stopping short of getting some of the stronger writers, like John, to help me pin him down and force feed him a piece of fruit.

The tone of *The Onion* in its early years, both in print and in the office, was playful. In the paper, deadheads popped up where ads should be, and little jokes were sprinkled everywhere like Sergio Aragonés' cartoons in *Mad*. *The Onion* was so silly, in fact, that we began to get word that some readers thought everything in *The Onion* was fake, including the ads. I can't imagine why people thought we would spend time making fake ads for real local businesses, but they did. To address this concern, we created a section in the back of the newspaper with entertainment reviews and movie showtimes, hoping this reality-based information would ground the publication and make it seem more real, therefore convincing readers the ads were real, and convincing advertisers their ad dollars weren't being wasted. I named the section "The Audio-Visual Club" after the group of nerds in my high school (me among them) who worked with the slide projectors and video equipment for the school.

The AV Club required someone on staff to call each of the movie theaters in town and painstakingly type out the showtimes from all the automated outgoing messages. It was a time-consuming task and it often fell to me. Sometimes, at first, I would get some of the showtimes wrong.

I got a call from an agitated reader one day.

"I looked up the showtime for a movie in *The Onion*, and I went to the theater and the movie wasn't showing!"

I didn't know what to say.

Then he laughed loudly and said, "You got me, *The Onion*! Good one!"

But, for the most part, the effort worked. The AV Club section made *The Onion* appear to be a more legitimate publication in the eyes of both readers and advertisers. It's become a respected online pop-culture review hub today.

Having legitimate entertainment reviews in *The Onion* meant we had to approach the movie, TV, and record companies and ask for press materials so we could get pictures to run with our articles. Once they had us on their mailing lists we started to get swag: things like keychains, beer cozies, headbands, stickers, and other garbage promoting all the new releases.

We despised this swag. To us it represented everything that was wrong with entertainment journalism. We realized this was how the big entertainment companies bribed reviewers into writing good reviews of their mediocre products, by wowing them with trinkets. We thought it was sad, and often ridiculed the items in the pages of *The Onion*.

We received a commemorative King Ralph plate promoting the John Goodman movie, *King Ralph*. We featured it on the front page being held by an important-looking museum curator. The headline:

"King Ralph Plate Sold At Auction." The subhead: "Bidding Expected to Exceed $30 Million."

Years later we would deride the movie further with the headline, "*King Ralph* Fails To Become Hip Retro Reference."

One day we received a box of T-shirts promoting the movie *Half Baked*, a stoner comedy starring Dave Chappelle and Jim Breuer. They were the most hideous T-shirts any of us had ever seen. They were bright purple with enormous green and orange letters that screamed "Get high!" and "Get drunk!"

Kelly decided the best way to satirize the existence of these awful T-shirts was to commit to wearing one of them every day for the rest of his life.

So, he took the entire box home, and every day from that day forward, he wore one of these shirts.

This went on for months. The shirts were such an eyesore, he became hard to look at. I found myself covering my eyes so I wouldn't have to see the top half of his body. (I suppose this made it easier for him to do his showing-a-testicle trick.)

Into the winter he was sure to wear the shirt over his sweater so it was always visible.

His roommates suffered most. They were slowly being driven mad by having to look at this hideous T-shirt every day and every moment Kelly was home.

The comedy experiment came to an end when Kelly came stumbling into his apartment drunk one night and passed out. His roommates took the shirt off his back, collected all the other shirts from his room, and torched them in a great bonfire.

At this time Kelly was *The Onion*'s assistant editor. Dan Vebber, the editor, was grooming Kelly to be his replacement. But as editor-in-chief, I would have the final say.

A new writer, Ben Karlin, was rising up through the ranks of the writing staff. He was a different sort of person. He had worked with *The Onion*'s business staff but wanted to be a writer. So, he came to writers' meetings and pitched ideas. He wasn't like the other writers. He was well-dressed, clean, and had good social skills—he didn't fit in at all. But he worked hard, and because he was good with people, I could see he was a good manager.

Unfortunately, a lot of the other writers didn't like Ben—maybe because he was different, or maybe they saw him as too ambitious. Some came to me privately and told me they thought his jokes weren't very good.

I wasn't concerned. I knew joke writing could be learned, and Ben was putting in the effort. Also, I had bigger concerns.

I had grand visions of transforming *The Onion* from small college humor rag to national newspaper parody. I wanted to stop publishing all the wacky college features and goofy contests we'd been doing and focus instead on the straight AP-style news. It was the purest, most outrageous expression of what *The Onion* was. It was our funniest stuff. I wanted to convert the entire newspaper into a complete package that might fool the casual observer into thinking it was a legitimate newspaper. It would have full color on the front page (we could afford it now), a weather map, stock reports, an editorial page, and a comics page. We would never break character and never wink at the audience.

Ben shared this vision, and helped me get other writers' stories in shape for this change. Kelly, on the other hand, came in one week after a four-day bender and slapped the entire issue together on Sunday afternoon, right before it was due. It was a funny issue—he was a good writer. But I knew we were never going to take *The Onion* to the next level with Kelly at the helm.

So, I hired Ben for the editor position.

I offered Kelly the opportunity to stay on as a writer, but he was angry, and quit in a huff. To my knowledge, he never went back to doing comedy professionally, which breaks my heart. His comedy was his art and his gift. He was like an Andy Kaufman or an Eric Andre. I should have wooed him better.

He did, however, leave Ben with a nice Kel-Dee card. On the front it said, "Congratulations on getting my job." On the inside it said, "You fucking prick."

10
LEGAL TROUBLE

It could have been the brashness of youth. It could have been our inexperience. Whatever the reason, we felt like we had nothing to lose at *The Onion*. We pushed limits. So many times I said to myself, "Well, this will be the last issue of *The Onion*."

Before I got involved with *The Onion*, the idea of edgy humor seemed cheap to me. There are arguments to be made for both clean and dirty comedy. Experienced standup comedians know working clean is more challenging than working "blue," but ultimately more accessible. Working blue, however, can get bigger, easier laughs. With *The Onion*, I allowed myself to experiment with the risqué and see where it would take me.

Tim and Chris led the way. They knew readers' expectations for a college humor publication: juvenile humor, shocking images, and pranks. They wanted to set themselves apart from the student-run newspapers on campus. They wanted to be rebels. And they wanted to get attention.

The Onion didn't pull off pranks, as a rule. We published a fake edition of *The Daily Cardinal* in the early 90s called *The Daily Tardinal* and didn't take credit for it. This stunt was straight out of the *Harvard*

Lampoon playbook. It garnered a little attention, but not much.

Tim and Chris had an attitude that encouraged behavior that was more radical than college pranks, more risky. Tim frequently said, "A little controversy is good for business." He knew it was a way to get noticed.

One way *The Onion* courted a little controversy that allowed me to dip my toes in the blue waters was swearing. Mainstream magazines and newspapers didn't print swear words in the 80s. They would spell the word *fuck* with an asterisk where the *u* went. Some of them still do! We decided we would proudly print swear words in *The Onion*, both in the bodies of stories and in headlines, as a way to mock traditional media as well as live up to the expectations of a college humor publication. This practice got us banned from distributing the paper in a lot of locations around Madison, but we believed being true to our brand was more important.

The nudity and other "adult" images we sometimes featured on the front page caught the notice of the Postal Inspector's office in Washington. We only had a handful of subscribers but the U.S. Post Office flagged our "Penis Fear" issue and one of Don Traeger's front-page penis shots ("Buck-Naked Man Stresses Importance Of Proper Schooling"). Pete and I faced potential fines and even prison time. There are apparently laws forbidding the mailing of parcels that have obscene material visible on the outside of the package. We had to figure out a way to affordably wrap issues of *The Onion* in black plastic like they do with porn on the gas-station magazine rack.

Nudity aside, I learned to enjoy creating edgy humor that made people uncomfortable. I stretched my comedy muscles by making fun of traditions and decorum that deserved to be made fun of, and this kind of humor felt edgy by being too soon or getting perilously close to hitting the wrong target.

Is there a line *The Onion* would never cross? If there ever was, we certainly crossed it. *The Onion* rarely crosses it now because it's learned its lessons. In humor nothing is off limits. You can make a joke as offensive as you want and target anyone or anything you want. But will people laugh? They will if the joke is funny and the butt of the joke has it coming. But they won't if the target is undeserving. They'll feel icky. Nobody (except a small minority of true sadists) enjoys humor that goes after an undeserving target. So, the only rule for satire: don't punch down; always punch up. That's the line.

I knew none of this in 1988.

Cousins Subs was a small, family-owned restaurant chain in the Madison–Milwaukee area in the 80s. Tim and Chris and their commission-only ad staff tried unsuccessfully to sell advertising to the place. They just wouldn't buy, even though they seemed like the perfect fit. Pizza and submarine sandwich restaurants were mainstays in *The Onion*. Tim and Chris didn't understand what Cousins Subs' problem was. So, *The Onion* started to browbeat them. In stories we dropped hints that Cousins Subs sandwiches were awful. We published a Snapshot that showed the different fitful bowel movements one could expect after eating a sandwich from Cousins Subs. In "Plebes," I drew a strip that featured six ways to get noticed by girls. One suggestion on the list was "car bomb Cousins Subs."

This barely veiled attempt to intimidate a small business into advertising with *The Onion*—encouraging a violent attack that put their minimum-wage employees at risk—definitely crossed the line. And it didn't work. The place still wouldn't run an ad. But I found out years later the owner of Cousins Subs had come close to filing a civil lawsuit against us for making a criminal threat. A lawsuit like that would have ruined us. We didn't have enough money to defend ourselves.

We eventually eased off our repeated assaults. After the incidents were long behind us and *The Onion* became successful, I felt a strange mix of pride and relief when Cousins Subs did indeed begin running regular ads in *The Onion*. They've grown to become a thriving restaurant chain in several states today.

Pete dealt with the advertisers. I didn't. Sometimes they seemed sketchy and I didn't want to predict what they might do. One of our advertisers, a bar down the street from *The Onion*'s office, always paid in cash for their little eighth-page advertisement. Even though paying by check was the norm, they ran their ad every week without fail, so neither Pete nor I thought much of it. Years later I heard the news that the owner of the bar had been indicted for laundering cocaine money.

In another close call with the law, Graeme Zielinski, one of our writers who actually had real-world journalism experience, used the names of his former high-school classmates in *Onion* stories instead of making up fake names, which was our policy. This wouldn't have been a problem except that he used the names for pedophile characters, exposing *The Onion* to potential libel lawsuits. I didn't fire Graeme for doing this; I just asked him not to do it again. He refused. After that I had no choice but to fire him.

In September 1995, *The Onion* ran a story about Gulf War syndrome, a condition affecting Gulf War veterans who came back from Iraq feeling unexplained fatigue, headaches, and skin disorders. The symptoms were believed to be the result of a suspected chemical-weapons attack by Saddam Hussein but no one knew for sure. Our headline suggested, "Gulf War Syndrome Caused By Idiots Who Join Army," a wince-worthy story that brazenly went after an undeserving target. The head of a small veterans group tried to organize a boycott against *The Onion* after that story ran, and he sent us angry letters for years whenever we wrote anything about veterans.

On the eve of the Academy Awards ceremony in 2013, *The Onion* called nine-year-old actress Quvenzhané Wallis "a cunt." It was a line that somehow got tweeted without proper vetting: "Everyone else seems afraid to say it, but that Quvenzhané Wallis seems like kind of a cunt, right?"

The backlash against *The Onion* for this tweet, even though it was quickly deleted, was greater than any I'd witnessed up to that point. It was an incredibly insensitive attempt at a joke. It would have been best to let the tweet be deleted, regretted, and forgotten. But the backlash was intense, mostly due to the fact that *The Onion* was far more widely distributed by this time.

A personal apology to the girl's family would have been appropriate (with luck, Quvenzhané herself never heard about it), but *The Onion*'s CEO, Steve Hannah, issued a public apology on *The Onion*'s homepage, suggesting that the writer responsible would be disciplined. The tweet was wrong, but Steve's apology was arguably worse, with cultural critics pointing out that the apology made *The Onion*, and the satire it purported to dish out, appear weak. Steve felt the apology was necessary to prevent advertisers from abandoning us. The apology was embarrassing, but I knew *The Onion* would survive it, just as it would have survived the tweet without the apology. The problem was, an apology on the front page of *The Onion* isn't funny. It's decidedly off-brand.

Even when *The Onion* crosses a line, the controversy it causes wanes in time. In the end the brand builds a reputation as an equal-opportunity offender that's unafraid to take risks. Tim was right about controversy being good for business. *The Onion* was poised to survive and thrive regardless of a mistaken tweet. We were a well-established brand by 2013—practically a cultural institution. We had a decades-long reputation to rest on. This wasn't like the early days of *The Onion* when nobody knew what we were and we had neither lawyers nor money to defend ourselves in court.

The office of the governor of Wisconsin threatened to sue us in 1989 after we had just turned one year old. For the October 31 issue of *The Onion* I planned a front-page story, "Gov. Proclaims November Masturbation Month."

Tommy Thompson was Wisconsin's governor at the time. He would later become George W. Bush's secretary of Health and Human Services. He would run a pitiful campaign for president in 2008 that fizzled as soon as people outside Wisconsin heard him speak (he sounded frightfully similar to Homer Simpson).

I needed a photo of Thompson for the story, so I called his press office at the capitol. I spoke with his press secretary, John Henkes.

"Who are you with?"

I could hear impatient fidgeting on the other end of the line.

"*The Onion*. We're a—"

"Oh, *The Onion*. I've seen it. No," he huffed. "I'm not gonna give you a photo."

I argued that I had rights as a constituent, and by law was entitled not only to an official photo of the governor, but also to run it in my newspaper. It was a public-domain image.

"Good luck with your project," he said, and hung up the phone.

With his refusing to help me, I was concerned we might not have any suitable graphic for the story. I hadn't been excited about using the official smiling portrait of the governor for the story to begin with, but I figured it was my only option. Now I had nothing.

In desperation I called the *Wisconsin State Journal*, the Madison-based daily newspaper. The photo editor there had a large file of photos of the governor and welcomed me to come by the office and pick one out. I went right over and was lucky to find a picture of Thompson speaking passionately at a podium—the perfect image for our masturbation story, and far better than the boring picture I would have gotten from John Henkes. Furthermore, the editor was happy to allow me to reproduce the photo free of charge, with no photo credit. This loaner would be off the books.

As I laid out the front page, I thought it would be a nice idea to add a fake photo credit. In very small type along the edge of the photo, I put "special thanks to John Henkes."

The next Tuesday, thousands of copies of the newspaper were distributed free throughout Wisconsin's capital city.

I promptly received an angry phone call from John Henkes. He threatened to sue, barking, "What kind of newspaper is this? This is not journalism!" He was right, of course. *The Onion* was not journalism. It was entertainment. But people weren't accustomed to a humor newspaper at that time. They thought newspapers were supposed to print actual news. He demanded a retraction.

I didn't want *The Onion* to get sued, but I also didn't want to appear gutless, so I printed a correction box in the next issue of *The Onion* on the inside front page. It said, "Correction: Last week *The Onion* erroneously reported that the governor had proclaimed November masturbation month. He had in fact proclaimed it Sodomy Month. *The Onion* regrets the error."

Not long after this close call, I received a knock at the *Onion* office.

I opened the door and was met by an important-looking attorney in a suit and tie, with greying temples and a humorless expression on his face. I thought he might be someone from the governor's office. But he wasn't. He had come to issue an all-new, unrelated threat:

"I understand you've reproduced a photograph of my client, Ginger Rogers, without her express written permission. I'm here to find evidence of that infringement and use it in a court of law when I sue you."

He barged into the office and demanded to see our archives.

I pointed to a disorganized pile of newspapers in the corner where we kept our back-issues.

As this attorney rifled through the newspapers, I felt weak in the knees. I was pretty sure *The Onion* had in fact reproduced a still from an old Fred Astaire–Ginger Rogers movie in an advertisement we'd made for a local hamburger place, Dottie Dumplings Dowry. We didn't know at the time that it's illegal to run a celebrity's photo in an advertisement without permission. Such use implies endorsement, and any lawsuit they might bring would be an open-shut case. *The Onion* would lose.

I thought, Oh well, this whole *Onion* thing was fun while it lasted.

After a few tense minutes that felt like hours, the attorney stood up from the back-issue pile and turned to face me.

"Gee," he said with a defeated sigh, "I had it on good authority you'd run that photo. But I can't find it."

I tried to conceal my relief. Apparently we hadn't run the photo after all.

"And you know what?" he said, "I'm glad! Because I think what you kids are doing is hilarious!"

He laughed a big, long belly laugh, and then recounted some of his favorite *Onion* headlines.

"Hello. I'm Kenneth J. Artis, attorney at law."

I didn't know if it was out of a sense of guilt or because he thought it would be fun, but in short order, Ken started to sound like *The Onion*'s lawyer.

Pete asked him how we could protect ourselves against such legal threats in the future. Ken said we needed a hold-harmless clause in the contract we asked our advertisers to sign. This would shift any responsibility from us onto the advertiser. Pete asked how much it would cost to have the contract redone. When Ken told him he would charge $75 to add the clause, Pete said we didn't have that kind of money. Ken told Pete to forget the money, and he rewrote the contract pro bono.

A beautiful relationship was born. For the next five years, Ken came into the office every Saturday night to review the current issue of *The Onion* before it went to press. He made sure we weren't printing anything that could get us sued. Furthermore, he offered to defend us against any bloodthirsty lawyers who tried to sue us out of existence like he had.

He defended us a lot.

Taco Bell threatened to sue us. They didn't like our front-page story, "Taco Bell Launches New 'Morning After' Burrito." This excellent article, written largely by Todd, described the "ContraceptiMelt," a new Taco Bell food item that, if consumed within 24 hours of intercourse, would terminate an unwanted pregnancy.

What chance did *The Onion* have against such a giant corporation? A pretty good one, it turns out. All it took was Ken talking to their lawyers for a few minutes and the lawsuit threats evaporated.

Ken was good.

I often got talking with him. He once explained to me that he was interested in something called "influence without power." It was all about being the dominant personality and getting your way in almost any situation. It sounded fascinating to me, and he was clearly a master of it. He disarmed people with his intellect, humor, and textbook knowledge of the law—or at least the way the law is practiced in the real world, outside of the courtroom. He was especially well versed in matters concerning freedom of the press and the First Amendment. His mellifluous voice was a cross between Perry Mason and Thurston Howell III. He was intimidating but lovable. On Saturday nights his unrestrained laughter while reviewing each week's issue of *The Onion* could be heard all the way down the hall.

Ken also served as a body double in *Onion* photos, typically whenever we needed a president or other official. He was the only person I knew who had a suit.

One day I received a phone call from a highfalutin Beverly Hills attorney who represented a famous female pop singer whose name I'm barred from revealing due to a nondisclosure agreement I signed. Apparently she was not a fan of our story, "Dying 13-year-old Gets His Wish, Will Pork [Famous Female Pop Singer]." In his defense, and hers, the article was awful. It made fun of her for being abused as a child, and quoted her as saying she wanted to perpetuate the cycle of abuse.

It was 1993. *The Onion* had not yet figured out the finer points of satire.

The attorney explained to me that he understood *The Onion* was a humor publication and that we had every right to make fun of his client because she was a public figure.

"However," he said, "she is very angry and very rich and may simply want to make a point by suing you out of existence."

I was beginning to understand this is how the law works in America. It has little to do with laws or justice; it has to do with who has the most money.

This situation seemed hopeless to me. I handed the phone to Ken and dropped my head.

Within just a few minutes, Ken and this Beverly Hills attorney were laughing together and sharing stories of their childhoods. At the end of the call, Ken signed up the other attorney for a subscription to *The Onion*.

Ken was a miracle worker.

I got some insight into how he works his magic when we did "*The Onion* Fine Dining Issue" in the fall of 1992. It was a "special issue" with fake restaurant reviews and articles about food, basically an excuse for the ad-sales team to convince restaurants to buy more ad space. This issue was a precursor of the kind of branded content that so pervades online entertainment like *The Onion* today. At the time, I was happy to produce articles about food regardless. *The Onion* always had excellent coverage of food, condiments, and area eaters.

On the front page of the Fine Dining issue was an interview one of our writers had done with a local butcher. The butcher didn't know he was talking to a writer from a newspaper, and certainly didn't expect their conversation to be printed on any front page. But in the interview he revealed which local restaurants bought his grade-C and grade-D meat. At first I simply thought it would be funny to feature an interview with a local butcher talking about meat. That was just the kind of non-sequitur information I liked in *The Onion*. But with this interview we had not only struck comedy gold; we had done some real investigative reporting.

When the Fine Dining issue hit the streets, we got an angry phone call from the butcher. He threatened to sue, claiming we had defamed him and that he would lose all his customers.

Though he was just a local butcher and not a powerful celebrity or corporation, this threat felt more dangerous to me than the bigger ones. His livelihood had genuinely been jeopardized. It also felt like we had in fact defamed him on some level by printing an off-the-record conversation, possibly in violation of some kind of journalistic ethics—a subject we knew absolutely nothing about.

I told Ken.

He said, "Give me $300 cash and I'll take care of it by the end of the week."

There was plenty of laundered cocaine money around the office, so I handed Ken $300 cash and found out later what he did: he visited the butcher shop. He complimented the butcher in his characteristic good-humored way about having seen him in *The Onion*. The butcher was visibly upset at first but Ken assuaged his concerns.

"When I saw that article," he said, "I said to myself, 'Now there's a butcher who tells it like it is. There's a butcher I can trust.'" And Ken proceeded to order $300 worth of meat.

The lawsuit threat disappeared and we never heard from the butcher again. Meanwhile Ken ate like a king for weeks.

11
THIEVES AND CRAZIES

Before his stint at *The Onion*, and before becoming a tax collector, Ken spent his time hunting down people who used Ginger Rogers' pictures without her permission and then negotiating settlement payments. He would get a percentage of each payment. It was like shakedowns on consignment.

I once asked him what life was like being a "jerk for hire."

He responded, "I'm actually a raging asshole for hire."

Now, he was our asshole. There wasn't a lot of money to be made pursuing thefts of *Onion* material, but Ken found what he could.

While we were struggling to get more exposure for our work, people often distributed our writing for free and without attribution. In the early days of the Internet, before there were many websites to visit, the way things went viral was through emails that got sent around and forwarded. By the mid 90s, people frequently copied *Onion* stories, without our name on them, and emailed them all over. We were getting priceless exposure to thousands of potential readers but no one knew it was our work.

Sometimes college humor publications would get the emails and reprint the stories. I had a soft spot for these people because they probably just didn't know any better. I asked Ken to scare them a little bit, insist they print an apology and give *The Onion* credit for the article, but no money need change hands.

Appearing as a formidable legal force in the comedy sphere positioned the *Onion* brand well, I thought.

Sometimes radio personalities got the emails and would read the stories on the air. Having spent much of my youth listening to the radio and producing radio comedy, I once thought being a morning-radio DJ was the job for me. And while I got a minimum-wage job at Wisconsin Pubic Radio that included a lot of on-air work, and I also made money on the side doing voiceover work for radio commercials, I never made the big bucks as a commercial radio personality.

It was therefore especially satisfying for me, if petty, to sic Ken on big-money celebrity DJs who ripped off *Onion* material.

The first ones to lift our work were Click and Clack, the Tappet Brothers. They read one of our stories in its entirety on their NPR show, *Car Talk*. The story was "Clinton Deploys Vowels to Bosnia, Cities of Sjlbvdnzv, Grzny to Be First Recipients." It was one of Robert Siegel's deadpan masterpieces, and one of our most viral emailed stories. Click and Clack laughed uproariously the whole way through it.

Car Talk exposed *The Onion* to the biggest national audience we'd ever reached, but Click and Clack couldn't tell their listeners where this story had come from because the email didn't give us credit. So, it did us no good.

I had a soft spot for these guys too. They said on air they wished they knew who wrote the piece. They wanted to give the proper credit but just didn't know who it was. We called them, and they were nice about it. They gave us full credit and a glowing review on the next episode of their show. We signed them up for a subscription to *The Onion*.

I never minded when DJs read our stories on the air if they gave us credit. This was free advertising for us.

Starting in 1989 we produced our own weekly minute-long radio show called *The Onion Radio News*, at first exclusively for local Madison rock station WMAD, and later for comedy networks like Westwood One and the American Comedy Network. I hired P.S. Mueller, who had worked as a DJ and newsreader on AM radio for years, to play *The Onion's* radio anchorman, Doyle Redland. He was the perfect voice for *The Onion Radio News*. He was authoritative, serious, and never broke character. When he read *Onion* stories, comedy sparks flew.

We occasionally produced fake ads and public service announcements to make a complete little news segment, sometimes adapting *Onion* print material, sometimes writing original sketches. Radio stations all over the world had access to this *Onion* material legitimately.

If they didn't pay for it, or if they removed our name and passed it off as their own (which happened far more often than it should have), that's when Ken would go after them. *Onion* readers were a big help in this regard. From all over the country, they would hear and sometimes record instances of radio DJs lifting our material without attribution, and they would alert us to it.

Ken would call the radio stations and explain the financial facts of life, the substantial penalties for purloining federally copyrighted work, and offer them an alternative payment. Generally the thieves were scared into writing a good-sized check.

One target of Ken's offensive strike was Mancow Muller, a DJ who, as of this writing, is still working in Chicago. He played a fake ad we'd produced at *The Onion*, a trailer for a children's movie called "Big Friendly Dog" which started innocently but got shocking really fast, moving straight into bestiality. He neither credited us nor paid us. In fact, on air he claimed he and his team had produced and written the bit themselves.

Thanks to a reader, we had a recording of the whole incident. Ken made his own recording, which featured the original *Onion* material, and then clips of Mancow's show in which the material was stolen.

Ken then interjected his own voice—at its most intimidating—explaining that the station's owners would have to settle up for the infringement.

Some of us got a glimpse into the dark side—the true raging asshole—of Ken in 1999. He came into the office to give the current issue of *The Onion* his legal review one Saturday evening, but the newspaper wasn't ready. He lost his cool, and unloaded at Robert, telling him, "You don't know who you're dealing with," and "I'll make your life a living hell."

Robert was scared. None of us had ever seen Ken like this before.

We found out later Ken was under a lot of stress. He had just come from a parking structure near the *Onion* office where he had destroyed a Porsche with a baseball bat. The damage was valued at $10,000. The vehicle belonged to his wife's boyfriend, whom he'd recently discovered.

Ken knew how to find a good lawyer, of course, and that lawyer wrote an excellent brief in Ken's defense. Ken received only a private reprimand from The Office of Lawyer Regulation. The case was ultimately dismissed.

Ken wasn't the only person who came storming into the *Onion* office fuming mad.

When we first moved into our basement office on Gilman Street, a rough-looking guy who reeked of liquor would come in on Friday and Saturday nights and harass us, asking, "What do you guys think you're doing here?"

He had his own keys to the office. He gloated about this fact, dangling the keys in front of us, saying, "Unlimited access." He came in often, and just stood around menacingly while we tried to work, asking us "You think this is your office, huh?"

We learned he had been the previous tenant. We asked the landlord to change the locks, but he didn't think it was a justified expense.

In 1994 we moved from our small basement office on Gilman to an eighth-floor office on State Street. The new office had more space. We had outgrown the basement; we were too often commandeering the shared conference room down the hall for meetings. Thankfully, our advertising revenue had steadily increased, and we could afford the additional space.

The security situation didn't improve, however. There was no lock on the main ground-floor door, since other retail businesses were headquartered in the same building, coincidentally other Madison comedy institutions: the Cheddarheads store, which sold foam cheese hats, Cheddarhead T-shirts and other merchandise, and the Funny Business Comedy Club, where Wisconsin's favorite comedian, Dave Grey, performed.

I was proud of our new office. I convinced Pete to let me spend some money to put a big *Onion* logo on the wall that could be seen outside the office's glass doors, and we hired a receptionist to sit at a large desk-like counter underneath the logo. Parts of our office, at least, were starting to look like a real fake-news organization.

The Onion didn't publicize its address but sometimes people figured out where we were and showed up. Other times, particularly after the bars closed at 2 a.m., when we were invariably still hard at work at *The Onion*, drunks wandered into the building and found our office. One night, Robert was working late on deadline when a drunken tourist came in from the street and hovered over Robert's shoulder while he was trying to write.

"What are you guys working on?" the drunk slurred.

Robert threw up his hands. "I'm trying to work here!"

Another person wandered in off the streets one day. He said he was hungry and wanted a sandwich. I thought he was a random homeless person, but upon closer inspection, I saw that he was Sean Mulheron, the mischievous and funny guy who just a few years earlier had been a promising *Onion* writer. He had fallen on hard times, and told me he was suffering from mental illness and cancer.

I bought him lunch. He confessed that he was angry. To me, he seemed unhinged. He was paranoid that *The Onion* had gotten rich off his work. I explained that all *Onion* writers were considered work-for-hire, which is standard in the industry. He came back a few days later, more upset and more hungry. He got belligerent, and I had to ask him to leave.

I myself was a raving loon at times.

In the days before digital printing, *The Onion*'s production process was laborious: we'd layout each story or ad individually in Pagemaker on our Mac lunchbox computer, transfer the files to a floppy disk, take the disk to the copy store to print the files, go back to the office and paste up the printouts of articles and ads onto large paste-up boards with hot wax, and then deliver the boards in person to the printing press.

I poured over the paste-up boards. I was obsessed with making *The Onion* as perfect as we could make it. So, typos or errors of any kind drove me mad. Because we didn't have our own laser printer, and because the printing-press deadline always loomed, to correct a typo or other misspelling, we would sometimes cut out the right letters from older printouts and stick the tiny squares of paper on top of any mistakes with hot wax.

One winter night, I was carrying the boards in a large flat box to my car to drive them to the printer. It was three o'clock in the morning, about twenty degrees below zero, and already past the printing deadline. The cover flew off the box and one of the boards blew away. I chased it through the snow. When I found it, I noticed a single 12-point *e* hot-waxed on top of it had come off. Because of the cold, the hot wax wasn't holding. I dug through mounds of snow with my bare hands for several minutes, raving like a lunatic trying to find that *e*.

In my saner moments, I discussed with Pete the possibility of investing more in the company.

By the mid to late 90s, *The Onion* had gotten to a level of success where we were financially secure, and it seemed like our continued growth was a good bet. But the writers, most of whom only came in the office for the weekly writers' meeting, were only making $15 a week. So, Pete and I agreed to reinvest all *The Onion*'s profits back into the company, and give writers real salaries, a 401K plan, and health insurance.

What this meant for me was that I was no longer receiving any profits from *The Onion*. This had been my primary source of income, and I could no longer pay my rent. So, I became homeless. I slept in the recording studio where we recorded *The Onion Radio News*, and I showered at the YMCA down the street.

I was volunteering with the Big Brothers Big Sisters of Dane County at the time. Now that I was homeless, despite the fact that I was supposed to be a responsible role model for my "little brother," Ben, his family took pity on me and let me stay in their unfinished basement for a few months. They had an old twin mattress I could sleep on.

During that time, that mattress was pretty much my home, and my sole worldly belonging.

One night I came home from working at *The Onion* at around 4 a.m., eager to get some sleep, only to find that their dog, Beaner, had peed on my mattress.

I didn't dare scream and wake up the entire house.

Actually, I wasn't really that upset. *The Onion* was finally getting some recognition. My work was reaching a wide audience, and I was content, feeling like my journey had finally come to some kind of fruition. Whatever emotional need I had been trying to satisfy with my lifetime of comedy output was finally being met. What might have been a low point in anyone else's life was, for me, a high point.

Part of being more widely recognized was that *The Onion* started to get hate mail at the office. Some of it was concerning.

After we published the story, "Pope Condemns Three More Glands," someone sent us a threatening letter in an envelope full of hundreds of the same clipping from *The Onion*: the picture of the pope's face from the article, cut out by hand hundreds of times. On a less creepy and more humorous note, some devout readers responded to the same article by pledging to have surgery to remove the offending glands.

There was one creepy guy from rural Wisconsin, a Christian fundamentalist, who wrote letters explaining that he didn't like some of our jokes; he felt they made light of both pedophilia and his religion. He wrote creepy hand-written letters to me, suggesting I should be killed by God. I never responded to the letters, but he kept sending them, and continued to make veiled threats on my life.

He showed up at the office one day. He looked liked someone auditioning for "stalker" from Central Casting. He was eerily lanky, with Charles Manson eyes and wild hair in need of a trim. He confronted me personally and told me the writing in *The Onion* was sinful and that we must all be punished. I countered that he had every right to say that and believe that, but he didn't have a right to threaten me or anyone else, or come to our office. I told him if he didn't like what was in *The Onion*, he could start his own publication, and we would compete in the marketplace of ideas.

He did. It was a mimeographed zine. He mustered the energy to produce only one or two issues, but the publication wasn't funny or entertaining. It was nothing more than a screed about how *The Onion* and I were evil, and that I deserved to die.

I filed a restraining order against him. The court case was unpleasant. He served as his own legal representation. It was like a bad comedy skit, where this stalker was cross-examining me on the stand, asking me what was so wrong about his stalking of me when I was, in effect, "stalking" his sacred beliefs in the pages of *The Onion*. He didn't seem to understand that promoting the death of an individual is different than comedy writing.

He lost the case and was barred from being in contact with me per the restraining order. Apparently, it had not been his first.

He later ran for some kind of regional government office in Richland Center, a town outside Madison. He didn't get a lot of votes, thank goodness.

The Onion's writing staff did a publicized book signing for our new book around that time. I was concerned the stalker would show up at the book signing and try to do some harm. I hired police to accompany us.

Not everyone who hounded us at the office wanted to kill us. Some just wanted to scare us.

We published an editorial by Donald Trump in 2013 headlined, "When You're Feeling Low, Just Remember I'll Be Dead in About 15 or 20 Years."

The next day, Steve received an email from Michael Cohen:

> Dear Mr. Hannah,
>
> I wish to call your attention to an article currently on your home page allegedly penned by Donald Trump entitled "When You're Feeling Low, Just Remember I'll Be Dead in About 15 or 20 Years."
>
> Let me begin by stating the obvious . . . that the commentary was not written by Mr. Trump. Secondly, the article is an absolutely disgusting piece that lacks any place in journalism, even in your *Onion*.
>
> I am hereby demanding that you immediately remove this disgraceful piece from your website and issue an apology to Mr. Trump. I further ask that you contact immediately to discuss.
>
> This commentary goes way beyond defamation and, if not immediately removed, I will take all actions necessary to ensure your actions do not go without consequence. Guide yourself accordingly.
>
> Yours,
>
> Michel Cohen
>
> Executive Vice President and
>
> Special Counsel to Donald J. Trump
>
> The Trump Organization

The Onion didn't respond or remove the article. Steve then began to get follow-up phone calls from Cohen. He couldn't seem to let the matter go.

At the time, I thought this was amusing, but it wasn't until 2016 when Donald Trump was revealed to have masqueraded as a fake publicist that I began to think differently about the matter. He called *Forbes*, identifying himself as John Barron. He called *People* as publicist "John Miller," pinching his nose to disguise his voice, boasting about Donald Trump: "He gets called by everybody in the book, in terms of women . . . He's got a whole open field . . . Actresses, people that you write about, just call to see if they can go out with him," and "He's doing tremendously well financially."

I looked back at the letter: there were favored Trump words like "disgraceful" and "disgusting," a demand for an apology, the clumsy, fifth-grade-level syntax. I wondered if perhaps it was Trump himself who had written the letter and was calling Steve in one of his other personas, formerly a fake publicist and now a fake lawyer.

The question remains open.

Boundaries always seemed to get pushed at *The Onion*. We pushed the boundaries to find our voice as a comedy brand. Sometimes it made people uncomfortable, even angry, and they pushed back. We were just being ourselves, living our mission, and saying what we felt needed to be said. We were compelled to process the world and all its insanity by turning it back on itself in the pages of our newspaper and website.

Sometimes it worked, and the zaniness of our lives fed our desire to create the craziest, funniest material we could. Our fan letters far outweighed our letters from kooks, lawyers, and stalkers, after all. We sometimes felt like we could do no wrong.

However, other times, when we tried to increase the scope of what we were doing, when we embarked on new projects to take *The Onion* to other media, like TV and movies, we discovered we could also fail spectacularly.

12
THE ONION'S FAILURES

Failure is the best teacher.

Yes, I'm one of those insufferable people who say there's no such thing as failure, only results. I failed a lot, and so did *The Onion*. We made a lot of comedy that no one thought was funny. It's how we got better.

In fact, the entire *Onion* writing system is built on failure. Hundreds of headline jokes are written every week at *The Onion*. Well over 95 percent of them fail to ever see print.

Quantity is a great way to achieve quality for the reasons I laid out in chapter seven. It has a fringe benefit too: when an idea doesn't pan out, you can often learn something from it.

A lot of my mistakes at *The Onion* related to leadership. As an introvert, I didn't know how to deal with people. Thankfully, I had a strong vision for the company and I pursued it passionately, which is the most important ingredient in good leadership. But aside from that quality, thrusting a loner like me into a position where I had to lead people at *The Onion* was a blueprint for disaster. My co-workers didn't understand me. I rubbed them the wrong way by coming off as unapproachable or just insanely work-focused. And I didn't know how to treat them. I was often dismissive and inconsiderate.

When Pete and I bought out Johnny's shares in *The Onion*, I said something that hurt his feelings during a meeting. I didn't intend to hurt his feelings—I was just stating a fact. I said that since he was a one-third partner and Pete and I were the other two-thirds, he had no power in the situation. He took my comment as an insult and lashed out by sabotaging the company. He locked all our computer files under a password on our single computer. We couldn't complete the week's issue until he unlocked it. He showed us who had the power. It was like factory workers staging a dramatic walkout.

A mutual acquaintance, a law student who had advised *The Daily Cardinal* on legal matters, stepped in to advise Johnny to turn over the computer files immediately, lest any deal he made be signed under duress and deemed void.

I had trouble dealing with Pete, especially in convincing him to invest money in things I felt were important. Occasionally I got through to him, like when I urged him to invest the $400 necessary to hire a web host so we could put *The Onion* online in 1996. But other times I couldn't make a persuasive case to him, like when I tried repeatedly to convince him to give the writing staff stock options as part of their compensation so they could have an ownership stake in the company. Negotiating and persuading were not my strong suits.

Feeling limited by my shortcomings, I spent much of my 20s reading books about how to learn social skills, increase my "emotional intelligence quotient," and become a better leader. I read *How to Win Friends and Influence People*, by Dale Carnegie. I turned it into a workbook, treating social interactions like homework. I would interact with people at a meal or party and then come home and write down what I felt I did right and what I did wrong, and compare my behavior with the principles in the book. I spent a year doing the difficult exercises in *Raising Your Emotional Intelligence: A Practical Guide*, by Jeanne Segal. The book changed my life. I listened to audio courses from Tony Robbins, Jay Abraham, and Earl Nightingale. I edited a series of lectures from a Total Quality Management seminar at Wisconsin Public Radio that gave me insights into how powerful good management could be.

In time, although I still had challenges, I became a passable leader of a small team at *The Onion*, despite the fact that I remained largely reclusive. I was determined to lead *The Onion* to bigger success, to branch out to other media.

I continued to pursue comedy endeavors outside *The Onion*, such as "Jim's Journal." (Eventually I stopped running the strip in *The Daily Cardinal* and moved it to *The Onion*.) I also did radio comedy. Jay Rath and I started a comedy troupe called the Radio Pirates, which included P. S. Mueller, local DJ Kathryn Lake, and others. We produced topical comedy sketches and uploaded them to the NPR satellite. A lot of stations downloaded the sketches and aired them, but we never took off, and never made any money at it. Our most successful production was a Halloween special, a parody of Orson Welles' "War of the Worlds" broadcast called *They Came for the Candy*. It still gets aired on public radio stations on Halloween from time to time.

Because I had sound-production know-how and wanted to reach the widest possible audience via whatever channels I could, I decided *The Onion* should release a comedy CD. I approached Todd Hanson to join the Radio Pirates for the project. He was on the outs with *The Onion* at the time. Both Rich and Dan had dismissed him for his inability to meet deadlines and what they felt was his overbearing behavior in the office. He was feeling depressed and uninspired. He was also injured, having recently thrown out his knee. I roused him from his crippled stupor and told him I thought he was a genius and that I wanted to work with him on some special projects. I wanted to lift him up, and bring his comedy magic to a wider audience.

He and I wrote several sketches for the CD project and also performed on it. We produced a parody song by the Pope, "Don't Have Sex." We did a spoof of a left-leaning community radio show hosted by two lesbians who take a caller who's looking for "hot lesbo action."

And we made a realistic-sounding presidential press conference where Bill Clinton whips out his penis. We also included a couple of Radio Pirates sketches on the CD, beefing them up to be edgier.

I decided to call the CD *Not For Broadcast*, since most of the material on it leaned heavily toward the juvenile and shocking end of the spectrum. My childhood friend Marce, now a professional illustrator, did the cover art.

I was proud of the CD. But we only sold a few hundred copies, and it mostly fizzled.

Todd and I jumped right from the CD to a TV project. I thought it would help build the *Onion* brand if we had our own sketch TV show. So, we embarked on writing sketches. We solicited help from other *Onion* writers and got good sketches from Andy Selsberg and Dan Vebber. Another sketch we used was written by a young Adam McKay, then a performer at The Second City in Chicago.

Archie Gips (then David Gips), who had produced a 70s nostalgia stage show in Chicago called *Saturday Morning Live* impressed and inspired me. Todd and I drove to Chicago and auditioned people from Archie's show and The Second City to be in the ensemble cast of our show. The final troupe was Brian Stack, whom Todd knew, Nancy Carell (then Nancy Walls), who would later become an *SNL* cast member and correspondent on *The Daily Show*. Other cast members were Matt Spiegel, Rich Hutchman and Andrea Gall.

Todd also had to be in the cast. I insisted on it. Among the accomplished, semi-professional actors we'd cast—all of whom were wonderful—Todd quickly emerged as the standout performer, even though he had very little experience. I always thought he missed his calling as an on-camera talent. He was without question a brilliant writer and satirist, but he had a stage presence akin to what they used to say about John Belushi: he captivated the camera; you couldn't take your eyes off him onstage.

Earlier, I saw Todd in a video Dan Vebber had made. It was a campy, low-budget sci-fi adventure with cardboard props and 70s-era

Dr. Who-type costumes. Todd played a space overlord of some kind, and despite the poor production quality and ridiculous dialog, he delivered a Brando-esque performance that brought me to tears. The dichotomy of the cardboard sets with Todd's brilliant acting was unreal. It was like watching Daniel Day-Lewis in *Plan 9 From Outer Space*.

The production of the TV show was a whirlwind. Ben Karlin and Michael Hirsch (Hal Mirsch) helped produce. Joe Garden and Kelly Ambrose created props. A local videographer and miracle worker named David Braga volunteered two weeks of his life to shoot the project by himself. And a local video-editing facility, ProVideo, put together the final show for us for cheap. Andy Wallman, an advertising copywriter and local improv performer, connected me with a lot of these resources. I'd later cast him in my first feature film.

The show was called *The Comedy Castaways*. The concept we came up with, which was executed in the short title sequence, was that the cast, green-screened onto a cartoon background like in a Saturday-morning show from the 70s, would get into a different fix every week and their only way out was to perform comedy sketches. In the first episode, they were on a boat at sea and fell into the ocean. Poseidon commanded they make him laugh. In the second episode, they got lost in a desert and ran into a mean cowboy named Black Bob who shot his six guns at their feet to make them dance and "do funny skits and plays."

Rich Dahm was a brilliant lyricist. He wrote the different opening title songs (both to the same tune), which the cast performed. Andrew Rohn, a local musician who had created the theme for *The Onion Radio News* and the music for *Not for Broadcast*, wrote and produced all the music for the show, which he arranged differently depending on the theme. The Poseidon episode had more pipe organ and brass, the Black Bob episode more mouth harp and fiddle.

Dan Vebber drew and animated the opening-title sequence. Keith made an animated version of his "H.J. Frogg" comic, which I planned to feature in the middle of each episode. The cast voiced all the characters.

One of the sketches featured Matt as Bill Clinton reaching out to every American citizen to personally make their lives better. The sketch focused on the first person on his list, Aaron A. Aaronson, played by Todd. Clinton helped him clean his house, get promoted at work, and find a date (Nancy) at a bar. In another sketch, a newsman (also Todd) faced a crisis of journalistic integrity when his boss (Andrea) told him he could no longer read the news on-air unless he removed the softball-sized toad on his cheek. Another sketch (written by Andy) featured an old man dying in the hospital (also Todd), telling his family in his strained last words that he wished he'd spent less of his life with them and more time at the office. Adam McKay's sketch was about a woman (Nancy) taking a creativity test who has no ability to be creative. Brian and Todd spoofed over-the-top dramatic characters in a Frankenstein parody where a mad scientist constructed homemade arts & crafts instead of a monster. In a runner, Rich Hutchman played a zookeeper obsessed with fuzz.

The Comedy Castaways was a big production for me, bigger than anything I'd ever worked on, and it strained my ability to lead people. I had a strong vision for the show, but Dan had a different vision for how to frame the concept in the title sequence. He began to take over the framing device in a way I didn't like and didn't think worked. He was filling a leadership vacuum I couldn't fill because I had too many other aspects of the show to manage. We butted heads one day, arguing about whose way was better. I wasn't sure how to resolve the situation. It pained me, because I can come to appreciate the look of Dan's cartoons and thought they were perfect for the show, but was emotionally attached to my vision, and it was difficult for me to compromise.

Stress was wearing me down. I was working constantly and made no time for a personal life or any kind of rest or recuperation.

I don't believe in magic or woo-woo stuff about dreams or astral projection. But that night, I had a wonderful experience. I had one of those dreams that feels more real than regular dreams.

It took place in a restaurant-bar, a nice, upscale place with a lot of dark wood surfaces. Sitting at the edge of the bar, waiting for me, was Steven Spielberg. We had arranged to meet. He was some kind of long-lost relative.

"Hi, Scott. I've been so excited to meet you," he said.

"Really?" I said.

"Yes, of course," he laughed. "What are you up to? Tell me everything. What do you do for a living?"

I told him at the moment I was trying to direct a TV show.

"Oh, I'm a director!" he said excitedly.

"Yes, I know," I said. "Everybody knows that."

"Well, let me give you some advice."

He pulled the barstool closer to me and put his hands on my shoulders.

"If you want to direct, you have to be direct."

The advice was so simple and elegant, I didn't know what to say. He must have read confusion on my face, because he elaborated, but just as succinctly.

"Use directives."

And the dream was over.

I went into the office the next day and found Dan working on his drawings for the title sequence.

"Dan, thanks for your input, but we're doing the opening title sequence my way. It'll look better."

He glanced up from his drawings and, without a trace of animosity, said, "okay." And we never argued about it again.

My dream-Spielberg had given me a new sense of confidence not only in the project, but in myself. I've never forgotten that dream. It still feels like a real-world experience I had.

We wrapped the TV show after two grueling weeks of uninterrupted 16-hour days. Like with the CD, I thought *The Comedy Castaways* turned out great, and was proud of the job everyone had done. The show was a lot like *Mad TV*, which would come out only a year later.

(There was no connection.)

I worked hard on the post-production sound for the show, and it sounded great. But when we aired the show on a local TV station—its big debut—they had a technical problem, and it was barely audible. Some people thought airing a comedy show that you couldn't hear was just another *Onion* prank.

The show was never seen after that.

I didn't know how to produce a TV pilot in the traditional way: going to Hollywood, getting a real production company, and having a studio fund the project. We had no hope of getting picked up by a network for our show the way we did it. This is how clueless I was about how the entertainment business worked. I only thought to do things outside the system.

What was wrong with these two projects? Why didn't they succeed? There are many reasons. The most important one, in my mind, is that they were off-brand. *The Onion* was a fake newspaper. *Not For Broadcast* was the type of spin-off project one could expect from an over-the-top college humor magazine. We had a Doyle Redland news bit on the CD, but it wasn't enough to make it fit the brand. Offensive sketch comedy was not what people wanted or expected from *The Onion*. I was trying to be outrageous, but I wasn't being true to my voice. I was more in line with the voice of *National Lampoon*.

The same problem afflicted *The Comedy Castaways*. The big difference between it and *Not for Broadcast* was that it was G-rated. A sketch TV show ended up working well for *Mad*. I believe that's because *Mad* was a different publication. It was for kids, so it was G-rated already (or, at worst, PG). And the magazine had different, modular features with different artists, so they looked and felt like separate things—a lot like a series of sketches. *The Onion* wasn't like that. I hadn't figured out how to be outrageous while also being in line with *The Onion*'s unique voice, which was still in the process of coming into focus. And I hadn't caught on yet to what that voice was.

A few years later, Todd and Robert and I started working on an un-titled *Onion* movie. Producers in Hollywood approached us with the idea that we should do a sketch movie. Apparently they hadn't seen *The Comedy Castaways.*

I left *The Onion* shortly after that, but Todd and Robert continued working on the movie. They sold it to Fox Searchlight. David Zucker, of the Zucker brothers who wrote and directed *Airplane!* And the *Naked Gun* movies, was one of the producers. After first offering it to me (I turned them down), they hired a commercial directing duo, Tom Kuntz and Mike Maguire, and the movie went into production.

One lesson Todd and Robert rightly learned from the CD and the TV show was that an ancillary *Onion* product should at least be news-based. So, they wrote a framing device for the movie involving an anchorman from "The Onion Nightly News" who faced a crisis of journalistic ethics.

The framing device was good, but altogether, the movie didn't work. Everyone involved at the studio and most of the staff of *The Onion* realized it would be a mistake to release the movie as is, even on DVD.

The Onion hired me back in 2005 partly to try to fix *The Onion Movie.* The main problem with it, I believed, was that the sketches weren't good enough. The overall narrative worked well, but the sketches weren't very visual and weren't funny. The opening of the movie was awful; front pages of *The Onion* were shot as if humor that worked in print would somehow work just as well if it's presented, as is, on the big screen. People don't go to the movies to read newspapers.

The first thing I tried to do was convince the studio to destroy the negative, and give us a budget to create a whole new movie. The staff and I brainstormed an idea called *The Americsons*, a mockumentary about a great, imaginary American family. The staff came up with some great material for the movie, and I conscripted comic mastermind David Rees to help me plot out the story.

The studio was excited about the prospect of a new *Onion* movie, but they didn't want to destroy the old *Onion* movie, which was the only reason I had proposed the new one. They had already invested $12 million into *The Onion Movie*, and they refused to throw it away. Instead of investing $1 million in *The Americsons*, they wanted to invest $1 million back into *The Onion Movie* to make it releasable. For their money, they wanted new, better sketches.

So, Todd and I started writing new sketches for *the Onion Movie*. We hired Scott Aukerman to help. *Comedy Bang! Bang!* was years away, but we knew him from being a writer on the HBO Show *Mr. Show with Bob and David*.

Scott didn't like working within the *Onion* system, so he bowed out after writing a couple of first drafts. Todd and I wrote a grand cinematic sketch about the Deathstronauts, a group of explorers who venture into the afterlife. They're celebrated by the entire world, like the Mercury Seven astronauts, but in the end they're just killed and then no one hears anything from them. Another sketch was a condensed spy-action movie with babies playing all the roles, not speaking any dialog except real baby talk and baby sounds. In the end, when the hero baby defeats the villain baby, the villain baby bawls his eyes out.

In the end, the Fox executives decided not to throw good money after bad. They decided to forego shooting any new sketches for the movie, and instead just re-edited the existing *Onion Movie* after I gave them some notes.

The movie was released on DVD with little fanfare, and remains a curiosity to this day. *The Washington Post*, one of the few mainstream outlets to offer any kind of review, called it "a straight-to-DVD suite of largely uninventive, charmlessly vulgar sketches."

In a fitting bit of irony that sums up the zany nature of the movie business, my primary goal had always been to kill *The Onion Movie* and prevent it from being released, yet I'm credited in the film as an executive producer.

13
DOING THINGS WRONG

If you Google "How to win customers," "How to attract Millennial customers," or "How to grow a business," you'll get lists of sensible suggestions for doing all of the above.

If you go down those lists, you'll see that *The Onion* violates just about every one of these best practices when it comes to its readers. It does so consistently, and in some cases purposefully.

How did *The Onion* grow into a successful brand by doing so many things wrong?

Let's go through the list.

1. Focus on solving a problem.

Solving a problem for a lot of people is always a good foundation for launching a business. *The Onion* doesn't solve a problem for its readers. Before *The Onion* came along, no one knew they needed it. Now that it's here, what problem does it solve? None, in the traditional sense. *The Onion* just spouts its opinion about current events.

If I had to gin up a problem that *The Onion* solves, I'd say it fills an emotional need for connection by bringing levity to people's lives, which all satire does. Just as writers of satire reach out to readers intellectually, trying to bond with them and find a sense of community, it can make the reader feel connected as well. The exchange treats them to another person's perspective, one that might make them see the humor in an unpleasant situation.

But that's a stretch. No investor would put money in a company trying to solve such a flimsy so-called problem.

2. Determine your unique selling proposition.

What's the one thing that *The Onion* offers that no one else offers? At first, almost no one offered news parody like *The Onion*. But now, *The Onion* is swimming in a sea of competitors offering the same thing.

The Onion strives to always be unique. The writing staff tries to tell jokes that aren't being told elsewhere, and also tries to tell jokes that get at the heart of a matter. But every day *The Onion* competes with thousands of excellent jokes being told on Twitter, or by Andy Borowitz in *The New Yorker*, or by late-night TV comics. It's becoming increasingly difficult to be unique.

It could be argued that all *The Onion* has is its idiosyncratic voice, just like any celebrity. But is that a selling position unique enough to build a brand and sustain a business?

3. Build a sales funnel.

The Onion tried a paid subscription model on its website once. It didn't work and we stopped doing it after only a few months. Most *Onion* readers were apparently happy to see an ad or two while reading *The Onion* for free online.

The Onion has merchandise for sale: T-shirts and mugs. In the past, we experimented with refrigerator magnets, hats, and trinkets of every kind. The stuff is funny, with T-shirts that say, "Owls Are Assholes" and mugs that say, "I Hate Whatever Today Is," "I Enjoy Branded Merchandise," and "Fuck Off, I'm Reading *The Onion*." These products have always made a little money, but not much.

Occasionally *The Onion* will release a book. Many of these books make the bestseller list, but they don't make nearly enough money to cover *The Onion's* expenses, and they don't compel customers to spend more money with us, like a good sales funnel should.

These are the only ways *The Onion* tries to make money from readers. There is no funnel.

4. Engage with customers online.

The Onion was the world's first humor website, but our website was like our newspaper: a one-way street. We never engaged with readers, never printed their letters, and never took their feedback. We liked when material connected with people, but we always wanted to be in control of the message.

We didn't want to engage with readers because it wasn't true to our brand. The brand was a faceless news organization. In order to parody the news media, we had to treat readers like slack-jawed layabouts who deserved only to be told what we claimed was the truth.

About ten years after *The Onion* went online, people started to talk about Web 2.0. The talk of the digital sphere was the importance of interacting with customers. The conventional wisdom was that users wanted to comment, have a conversation, and be involved in companies' decisions. Any company that didn't engage with people like that would be left in the dust.

I bristled at the idea. The primary conceit of *The Onion*, printed on its masthead for years, stood in stark opposition:

> *The Onion* neither publishes nor accepts letters from its readers. It is *The Onion*'s editorial policy that the readers shall have no voice whatsoever and that the *Onion* newspaper shall be solely a one-way conduit of information. The editorial page is reserved for the exclusive use of the newspaper staff to advance whatever opinion or agenda it sees fit, or, in certain cases, for paid advertorials by the business community.

We continued that policy, and our online business grew every year, despite resisting the urge to play the Web 2.0 game.

In 2008 we hired Baratunde Thurston to be *The Onion's* first digital director. He signed us up for Twitter and began managing our other social media, encouraging us to embrace the realities of this new interactive medium. *The Onion* continued to essentially ignore readers, but we at least took a gingerly step in the direction of engagement.

The Onion continues to resist Web 2.0 to this day. There are still no comments on *Onion* stories (except on Facebook, where I've never seen *The Onion* respond). On Twitter *The Onion* simply tweets out headlines, and never replies. So, in many ways *The Onion* is still a one-way conduit of information, the truest manifestation of its character.

5. Give customers what they want.

Here's an outrageous strategy: don't just berate customers and refuse to interact with them, but also purposefully take things they love away from them.

There have been plenty of features in *The Onion* I thought were good and that readers liked. There were other features in *The Onion* that readers adored but that I thought were beneath us. Things like "Soap Opera Summaries," the silly, non-newsy deadheads, and certainly "Drunk of the Week."

For most of *The Onion's* first 15 years, we had no way to know, with any certainty, which features people liked and which they didn't. We had nothing like the online tools creators have today like social media, direct feedback, and heat-map analysis of user data. In the early days of *The Onion*, all we had was our horse sense. The only clues available were the reactions of our peers, our contributing writers, the ad staff, or any random word we picked up off the street from friends, acquaintances, or comments we might overhear in coffee shops and bars.

From that, we knew "Drunk of the Week" was the most popular feature in *The Onion* in the mid 90s. The feature was created when select *Onion* staff would go out on State Street after the bars closed on Friday or Saturday night and find a drunken college student stumbling out of a bar. They would conduct a brief interview as they were able, given the subject's inebriated state, and take a picture of the drunk holding a sign that said, "Lord Help Me! I'm *The Onion*'s Drunk of the Week and I Am Dumb."

Comedy crowds are tricky beasts. They like crowd-pleasing jokes, obviously. But crowd-pleasing material is not usually the most sophisticated. Crowds will laugh at shock humor without subtext. They'll laugh at clichés. They'll laugh at the easiest jokes you can throw at them. Audiences like low-hanging fruit. They don't have refined tastes.

I admit I had no desire to provide highly sophisticated or intellectual humor in *The Onion*. Far from it. I wanted to present humor that would make people laugh so hard they would cry. And I was beginning to learn the secrets of how to do that. One way was to exceed people's expectations.

When I decided to discontinue "Drunk of the Week" after redesigning *The Onion* as a serious newspaper parody and not a wacky college humor publication, I got some pushback from Pete and the ad staff. And I got a few complaints from readers. But it didn't last long.

I believed I knew what readers needed; I didn't necessarily care what they wanted. They appreciated the sharpening of the brand as *The Onion*'s voice became clearer, and they soon forgot about "Drunk of the Week."

Another popular column I killed was one I penned myself.

We ran an editorial comprised of nothing more than the verbatim lyrics of the song "I Can Love You Like That" by the 90s R&B group, All-4-One. I enjoyed 90s R&B music and thought the lyrics were funny when written out in prose.

A sound engineer I knew, Steve Gotcher (who posed for many *Onion* photos as Local Man Don Turnbee), was producing an album for a local R&B artist named Butterscotch. I came in the studio once when Butterscotch was laying down vocal tracks. Steve was at the mixing console. The lights were turned low, to set the mood, and Butterscotch was hidden in the darkness of the recording booth while a slow, sexy beat and synthesizer played on the speakers. His vocal track was just moans.

Steve turned to me with a dyspeptic look on his face and said, "I hope he's not jackin' off in there."

Butterscotch then began speaking in an oddly prosaic—almost robotic—way. He said, "Okay, girl, take your clothes off now. Your underwear too. That's right. Place it on the dresser."

It was one of the funniest and least sexy things I'd ever heard.

I wrote a column by an R&B-inspired character who talked like this, making sexual come-ons in a clunky way. Mike Loew found a photo in an old yearbook from a Milwaukee high school that someone had donated to us. The guy was leaned back in the photo and had a come-hither smile. Mike gave him a modern, hip-hop haircut in Photoshop and soon we had the perfect picture for the character of Smoove B.

Smoove B became so popular, he started to become the only thing I heard about when I would hear people talk about *The Onion*. The character was funny, but one-note, always telling his woman how he'd make love to her, or begging her to come back. After just a few columns, I delighted in killing off Smoove B, treating readers like children who had had too much dessert.

6. Be genuine.

Marketing experts nowadays will tell you Millennials especially like when their brands are genuine.

The writers of *The Onion* are never genuine with readers. They never speak as themselves; they only speak in the affected, AP-style news voice of *The Onion*. Everything they say is disingenuous. Furthermore, all the news stories are fake.

It was more important to me that *The Onion* be true to the character of its brand than to be genuine. The character was the bumbling authority archetype. It had to be self-important, smarter than you, and played straight. But at the same time, everything it said had to be ridiculous.

All we ever did was lie to our readers.

7. Know your customer.

Okay, I'm having a little fun with you here. A big part of what's made *The Onion* a successful brand is that we know who our customers are, and who they aren't.

The Onion has two classes of customers: one is its readers, the other is its advertisers.

Advertisers are the customers who pay the bills. In that sense, they're our real customer. And with them, *The Onion* plays by the rules: it treats its customers exactly the way you're supposed to; it provides a valuable service, delivering the eyeballs of millions of customers to focus on the advertisers' products.

When *The Onion* began selling advertising in Madison, Wisconsin, we could tell them we were the only humor publication on campus. That was our unique selling proposition. Tim and Chris hoped to demonstrate that *The Onion* could reach local businesses' target demographic by running coupons on the bottom three inches of every issue, even on the front page. *The Onion*'s coupon section could be cut out and used as a coupon book.

When advertisers counted the coupons that came into their stores and then compared the volume to coupons from other local newspapers, they got an accurate idea of *The Onion*'s value.

But even with the coupon book, there were inherent challenges with this positioning. First, *The Onion* was a new thing, a humor newspaper. People had to be told what it was. Had it been a traditional humor magazine, people would have understood. Second, there was that problem I mentioned where readers thought everything in *The Onion* was fake, including the ads. The AV Club was our customer-driven solution.

Eventually, advertisers figured it out, and saw that advertising in *The Onion* actually reached people. *The Onion*'s ad staff today can confidently position *The Onion* as a unique offering that has a devoted following of millions of readers, and they can use incredibly detailed analytics to show that advertising in *The Onion* gets results.

The Onion engages with its advertisers, and gives them what they want.

From the beginning, *The Onion* made it clear to its readers that they weren't important to us. We called them dumb, we called them ignorant dullards, and we forbade them to talk to us. When *The Onion* was redesigned with full color on the front page and repackaged as a complete newspaper parody, a large front-page editorial explained, "This Attractive, Colorful Redesign Is for Our Advertisers, Not You."

But if *The Onion* treats its advertisers like truly valued customers and readers like crap, why did we get so many fan letters when *The Onion* first started to become nationally known, with readers screaming, in all caps and streams of exclamation points, expressing their deep love for *The Onion* and their willingness to do anything for us? These are the kinds of raving fans every business dreams about.

The conventional wisdom concerning customers is to listen to them, take their feedback, and let them feel personally invested in the quality of the product or service so they're inspired to become fans.

I knew this. I had studied W. Edwards Deming's Total Quality Management. But *The Onion* made me feel bold. Tim and Chris encouraged me to toss out conventional wisdom about how to treat customers and shoot for a higher goal: living out the most outrageous version of our brand identity. This is a more powerful marketing strategy. It not only satisfies the six items on the list above, it does so much more. For *The Onion*, it spurred the growth of not only raving fans, but rabid fans, fans who would proselytize about *The Onion*, and show up for us when we needed them. They alerted us when people stole our material, or when people said unkind things about us. I used to call them our "private Christian army."

So, the question remains, why did readers like being berated, having things taken away from them, being lied to, and being ignored?

Because it's satire. They knew we loved them. Even though we used a character voice, they knew we were honestly communicating our feelings about the world to them. We spoiled them with tons of free, funny material that never seemed to stop. They liked having their favorite things taken away from them because while audiences love easy jokes and red meat, they love even more a confident entertainer who can leave them wanting more, and then excite them with something new and better.

Readers of *The Onion* enjoy a game of peek-a-boo with a stuffy old newsman telling them funny lies. The character of *The Onion* blusters and bloviates like Oz, but readers know the kindly satirist behind the curtain is going to take them home in a balloon. They like being ignored because it's funny. Readers are routinely ignored by the mainstream media, but the mainstream media would never admit this. When *The Onion* admits it, readers feel a kinship. "*The Onion* gets it," they think. They feel like *The Onion* captures that uneasy feeling they get when they interact with the mainstream media. They feel like *The Onion*, in a strange way, is the only one telling them the truth.

14
PRESS RELEASES, SCHMESS RELEASES

The Onion was on the map by about 1995. But it was a small map. Our total circulation was similar to that of a small-to-medium-sized city newspaper. We had four editions in print: Madison, Milwaukee, Boulder, Colorado, and Champaign-Urbana, Illinois. That meant we were on people's mailing lists. We received press releases for every random thing that every marketing professional was trying to publicize.

We were notified when Post introduced Waffle Crisp cereal. We were alerted when a local church group was planning a food drive or pancake breakfast. We got every press release from every political campaign.

Usually, we threw them away. But one day we received a press release from the campaign of the incumbent medical examiner in Dane county. Whoever wrote the press·release must have had newspaper experience, because they wrote an entire intact editorial column endorsing the candidate. Like I had done with "Jim's Journal," they provided paste-up ready copy for a lazy newspaper to simply cut and paste into their next issue. Much like the packaged advertorials local TV news stations air, this was a glimpse into the surreptitious reality of print editorials: marketing professionals barrage newspapers with ready-made opinions, and newspapers just cut, paste, and print. Filling several pages of broadsheet newsprint with copy every week—or every day for some papers—is not easy. Why hire writers? Press releases are free.

The editorial, titled, "Keep Wopeska Coroner," was unwittingly funny enough that I decided to run it as an article in *The Onion* verbatim. It ran as one of our "wacky character" editorials. I thought it was one of the funnier editorials we'd ever run. It was played perfectly straight, of course, and concerned an issue not a single *Onion* reader cared about. For me, there's not much funnier than that. It had the added bonus of shining a satirical light on the fact that unscrupulous news sources often present editorials crafted by publicity people.

Yet, even though *The Onion* had grown to be bigger than a typical college humor publication, we continued to struggle with our lack of notoriety. We thought we were doing good work and wanted more people to see it. All these press-release mailing lists knew about us. Local advertisers were buying more space in *The Onion*. Readers knew and liked us. But we wanted more. I wanted to be noticed by the whole world. Before the Internet, I wanted to go viral.

This was a marketing challenge.

Fortunately, Ben Karlin had some business savvy, and knew a little about marketing. He suggested *The Onion* send out press releases. If cereal companies and county coroners can solicit publicity from newspapers, why couldn't *The Onion*?

So, under Ben's direction, we wrote press releases and sent them out. When *The Onion* came out with a new issue, we sent out a press release. If *The Onion* wrote something particularly newsworthy, we sent out a press release. When we released our CD and our TV pilot, we sent out a press release.

And no one wrote about us.

It was a long shot. Having been in receipt of hundreds of press releases myself that I threw away as soon as I opened, or, more commonly, threw away before I even opened, we should have assumed any press releases sent out by *The Onion* would be similarly discarded.

Meanwhile, whenever we got into mischief like with the Wisconsin governor, or when we wrote about a certain female pop singer and almost got sued out of existence, these things made the news.

The idea of outrageous marketing was starting to become clear to me. When we pushed the boundaries of what was acceptable for a newspaper, we lived out our identity as a strange mix of college humor publication and news source, and people talked about it. The more we hit those buttons, the more the media talked about us. And the more we lived up to our growing reputation as a fake newspaper, the more we were able to hit those buttons in bigger and louder ways.

We learned that to get attention in the press was not to send out press releases; it was to do things that were press-worthy.

We pushed this strategy to the limit, working to heighten the serious tone of our news for maximum contrast between our straight face and our silly antics.

Our growth and expansion itself became the story. After we launched our website, *The New Yorker* wrote a nice review of us. TV stations started calling, wanting to come to our offices to profile us. When we published our first book, we were invited on a slew of TV and radio shows.

As we continued to sharpen our focus and create new products that accentuated our brand identity, another strange phenomenon began occurring aside from media attention, and it would get even more people talking about us, helping spread organic word-of-mouth about *The Onion* further and wider than ever.

The first time I experienced this phenomenon was after our story, "Chinese Woman Gives Birth To Septuplets, Has One Week To Choose." The story explained that, according to Chinese law, the new mother would have to throw all her babies except one off a mountaintop.

We received a letter from a woman in the Midwest who was praying for those babies and wanted us to know she had reached out to her prayer group for additional support. She assured us Christians all over the country would be praying for those poor babies.

Someone thought a story in *The Onion* was real!

Later that year, we published the story, "Homosexual Recruitment Drive Nearing Goal," which explained that the National Gay & Lesbian Recruitment Taskforce had successfully converted hundreds of thousands of straights into the homosexual lifestyle that year. None other than Fred Phelps, the "God Hates Fags" guy, now deceased, pointed to that article as incontrovertible evidence that homosexuals were infiltrating our schools and corrupting our children. He put a link to our story on his official Westboro Baptist Church website.

To address this particular situation, I approached our webmaster, Jack Szwergold, who had informed me about Fred Phelps linking to us. The Internet was new at the time. This was 1998, and Jack was my answer man.

"Jack, how do links work?"

"Well, on his website, he has a hyper-link that you can click on, and if you did, it would bring you to *The Onion*'s page."

I thought about the idea for a moment.

"I see. Could we reprogram our website so that if someone came to us from his page, instead of going to the Homosexual Recruitment story, they would go somewhere else instead?"

"Hm. Yeah, I think there's actually a way we could do that."

We smiled at each other.

"Let's do it."

The only step remaining was to select the destination for the hapless "God Hates Fags" fans.

We could have sent them anywhere, to a water-sports porn site or a Satanist fundraising page. But there weren't a lot of websites online. We decided to send them to a simple *Onion* story: "Church Cancelled Due to Lack of God."

The Onion ran a story headlined, "Planned Parenthood Opens $8

Billion Abortionplex," and a congressman from Louisiana took it seriously, citing it as evidence that Planned Parenthood was out of control with its "wholesale" abortions. And he wasn't the only one. Hundreds more were fooled when *Onion* readers put up fake Yelp reviews for the Abortionplex, broadening the unintended prank.

In 2012, *The Onion* named North Korean Dictator Kim Jung Un the world's sexiest man alive. The official news agency of China re-ran the story in its entirety, even adding additional photos of the sexy dictator to augment the glowing profile.

China was fooled again by the *Onion* story, "Congress Threatens To Leave DC Unless New Capitol Is Built." According to the story, the Congress wanted a retractable dome and luxury boxes for VIP seating, otherwise they would take their business to a different city— one that would treat them better, like maybe Memphis. An elaborate Adobe Illustrator graphic showed the proposed new design with the retracting dome. Despite its absurdity, one of the largest circulation newspapers in the world, the *Beijing Evening News*, re-printed the story verbatim—including the bogus graphic.

When they realized they had published a story from a comedy publication, the editors printed a retraction in the next edition of the *Beijing Evening News*. It said, "Apparently, there are newspapers in America that print lies!"

A Tumblr blog called "Literally Unbelievable," put up by an *Onion* reader, continues to catalog instances of *Onion* stories being taken seriously. The subreddit AteTheOnion does the same.

A wonderful side effect of all this erratum is that it enhances the entertainment experience for the readers who are in in the joke. They get to enjoy another layer of the humor, a layer of street art, an impromptu prank.

When people who should know better mistakenly believe *The Onion* is factual, news of their witlessness spreads and *The Onion* gets a lot of attention. But this was only one of many ways *The Onion* leveraged its brand identity, honed it, and continued to get more publicity.

15
OUR DUMB CENTURY

I prefer to be the dumbest person in the room. Intelligent people excite me. Their wits lift me up and make me unconsciously strive to be smarter.

One of the things that's impressed me most about the writers who were drawn to work for me at *The Onion* was their intelligence. These were people who had genius-level IQs. Most of *The Onion*'s writers were easily MENSA candidates. By the same token, some of them couldn't seem to show up to meetings on time. Most were emotionally fragile, like me.

But the quickness of their intellects was undeniable. And, as someone who has consistently tested pretty average, I found it a wonder to behold. Robert Siegel told me his IQ was above 150, and I believe it. His relentlessly curious mind was always digging for the truth in every situation. John Krewson didn't need to tell anyone his IQ score. Anyone who spoke to him for a few seconds knew immediately that he was in Garry Kasparov territory. Beyond that, he was a treasure trove of arcane knowledge. He seemed to know everything about everything. And if he didn't, he could bullshit his way through it so convincingly that you'd believe he had a PhD in the subject.

Krewson talked fast, with an almost robotic precision. His mind was like a comedy computer. He had the kind of calculating intellect that surely confounded high-school bullies in the small Wisconsin town where he grew up, especially since John had been a high-school athlete and was in fact the *Onion* office's reigning arm-wresting champ.

Tim Harrod was a comedy savant. He seemed to have an encyclopedic knowledge of every joke ever told on any comedy show or written in any comedy publication. I had never seen him stumped in that regard. Before the Internet, this was a handy skill.

Mike Loew knew everything about the governments of the world. If you named a country, he could tell you what was going on politically in that country at the moment, and give you a good overview of the country's political history. This wasn't even his subject in school. He got his degree in creative writing. His worldly knowledge was instrumental later when we wrote a parody of a world atlas, *Our Dumb World*.

David Javerbaum was a friend of Ben Karlin's from Brookline, Massachusetts who'd gone to Harvard. He'd been contributing jokes and stories to *The Onion* before any of us met him. One was headlined, "Clinton Blown Away," with the subhead, "By Delicious Flavor of Trident Gum." In *The Onion*, the story was accompanied by a blurry photo of Secret Servicemen scuttling Clinton into a limousine. DJ, as he's known, had a reputation that preceded him. His quick, exacting speech made him a sort of blue-blood Northeastern John Krewson. He was the only writer at the time who had written for both the *Harvard Lampoon* and *The Onion*.

DJ aced his SATs—a perfect score. This was something I'd never heard of before. As someone who had flunked out of high school and never even taken the SATs, I was impressed.

He came to Madison to visit Ben and meet the staff at *The Onion*. He, Ben and I talked about the idea of doing an *Onion* book. There were a few ideas being tossed around. I had an agent who represented me for my "Jim's Journal" books, but *The Onion* didn't have an agent yet. Still, a book was a natural outgrowth of *The Onion*, and I felt it was something we should pursue. We weren't online yet, but we were already working on a comedy CD, a TV pilot, and a radio show.

I wanted to do everything.

DJ suggested it would be a good idea to do a book that looked back at the history of the twentieth century through the pages of *The Onion*. This was the mid 90s, after all. I knew Robert was a big fan of *New York Times* books like this, and so was I. Who didn't like books of old newspaper front pages? I ruminated on the book idea more, talked to some of the other writers, and we began working on the book.

We were encouraged by a special theme issue we'd done. Much like our parody of *The Daily Cardinal* from a few years earlier, in 1996 we produced an authentic-looking 1896 issue of *The Onion*, in black-and-white, with old-time fonts and almost no photos in the issue save for a crude daguerreotype image of a crashing flying machine on the front page.

The 1896 issue had been tremendous fun to make. Maria and John especially had a knack for writing news copy that sounded like it belonged in newspapers from a century ago.

The issue gave *The Onion* one of its proudest early moments of national exposure when Bob Odenkirk requested to use a copy of it as a prop on *Mr. Show with Bob and David*. The episode began with him onstage idly reading the 1896 *Onion* without explanation, waiting for David, who was late to the show opening.

But a book was a different project altogether. We knew we would have to do double the work we normally did every week to produce both *The Onion* and an *Onion* book. *The Onion* itself was already a 70-hour-a-week job for many of us. We knew a book of *Onion*s from the past was going to be an enormous, punishing task.

What's worse, by that point in my life, I was well versed in my own inadvisable method for tackling large projects: ready, fire, aim. I always wanted to get the project started at all costs, because I knew "R&D"

could go on forever if you let it. Most people I'd worked with enjoyed talking about things, planning things, and considering things. I just wanted to make things. This usually resulted in a terrible lack of planning and a lot of wasted time.

But I also believed a little bit of chaos, especially in the beginning, was a good way to discover what was working about a project. For the *Onion* book, like with the *Onion* newspaper, we wrote hundreds of headlines. We went decade by decade, starting with 1900 through 1910. The Internet was too young to be of much use to us in the beginning. There were one or two books around the office that we had either picked up from the library or that someone on staff brought from home. One indispensable resource for us was an almanac that listed news events and trends at various points in American and World history.

I cautioned the writers not to do too much research. It wouldn't do us any good, I thought, to have stories about obscure historical events no one knew about. In fact, I encouraged them to come up with as many ideas as they could before doing any research at all. This is how we were able to tackle tentpole subjects that almost anyone could remember from the history of each decade. In the 00s and 10s, it would be the assassination of President McKinley, WWI, and random things like the Sears, Roebuck catalog, which we all remembered from reprints that seemed to be on everyone's coffee table growing up.

Funny headlines began to emerge from the process, like "McKinley Attacked by Wild Boar," "600,000 Killed in 4-Inch Advance on Western Front," and "Sears, Roebuck Plead 'Not Guilty' to Pornography Charges," due to their scandalous etchings of women in full-bodied undergarments.

The tone and style of the book, such as it was slightly different from *The Onion*, began to take shape. It had another layer of ironic distance or lack of awareness because it was an anachronism. It had another layer still from our benefit of hindsight. The historical headlines in the book, it seemed, could carry even more subtext than modern *Onion* headlines.

Each decade proceeded at pace, and we began to see what this book could be.

We had arguments early about the format of the book. I wanted each page to be a reproduction of a front page of *The Onion*. The writers—Todd especially—believed that because this was a book, there should be writing in it, not just front-page headlines. I argued that there would be writing, that the stories would be featured on the pages, at least as far as they went, but they would disappear at the "jump" like on real front pages. Todd and the others hated this idea. They wanted full stories in the book. I couldn't abide that idea. I knew it would be a mistake to show other pages besides front pages that would essentially just be blocks of copy. I knew from my experience publishing cartoon books that people like a humor book they can browse. Also, if this book was to be a parody of "great front pages" books, it should only have front pages in it. In those books, they don't show page A13 where the story from the front page continues. This was a heated conversation that went on intermittently for days.

At long last, a compromise was developed. We would feature full stories in the book, but we would violate verisimilitude by having the stories conclude on the front pages. No newspaper does this, but we agreed we had the poetic license to do it, and no reader would care. If the newspapers looked authentic, this inaccuracy would be overlooked.

Another issue we had to confront was the type size. If a front page of a newspaper were reduced to a reasonably sized book, the body type would be far too small to read. We used another poetic license to solve this problem. The type in our book would indeed be extremely small, especially in the early part of the century—and many beta-readers expressed concern about this—so we increased the size just barely enough to be readable. If the front pages were enlarged to actual size, our body type would have been absurdly large. But again, they looked authentic, so no one cared.

Shortly after we got started working on the book, I collected our best jokes and wrote brief stories for a WWII page spread ("Dastardly Japs Attack Colonially Occupied U.S. Non-State" and "Coca-Cola Named Official Soft Drink of Second World War." I put together another spread with stories borrowed from our 1896 issue. I came up with a title, *100 Years Of Headlines from America's Finest News Source*, and sent the two-page proposal to our new agent, Daniel Greenberg. He got us a contract with Hyperion, the Disney-owned book publisher. I met the editor there, and we were off and running. They paid us an advance of $100,000. Neither the writers nor I received a cut of the advance for working on the book; we only received our regular pay, despite the fact that we were doing double duty on the newspaper/website and the book. All the money went to *Onion, Inc.* Pete and I fought about this, but we had our deal, and he had the final say about how the money was spent.

The editor gave me a deadline for delivering the final manuscript. Later, we would steamroll right past that deadline without noticing.

Once the headlines started coming in, I began assigning stories. I assigned one of the first stories to Tim for the San Francisco earthquake headline, "Earthquake Marks Least Gay Day in San Francisco History." He turned in a two-paragraph story that had a couple of gay puns in it.

Onion writers were spoiled in those days. Robert and the editors before him unfortunately inherited a practice I had pioneered which was to completely rewrite writers' stories when they came in in rough shape. This is something that happens on sitcoms a lot. A staff writer will write an episode of a show, and then the head writer will rewrite it. It seems easy for an editor to do this because it's less trouble than having to painstakingly explain to the writer what's wrong with the draft. However, rewriting consumes just as much of the editor's time and energy, and worse, erodes the relationship between editor and writer. Eventually, writers get lazier and lazier, and hand in work that's woefully sub-par because they know the editor will fix it.

I rewrote the earthquake piece as a full-length story, but took Tim's pun take on the story and ran with it, writing the entire story (in the antiquated style of early-twentieth-century newswriting) as a relentless volley of puns and other wordplay using synonyms for "gay" as if the writer of the article didn't realize it meant "homosexual." I recognized this as the central joke of the headline, so I knew the story would have to deliver on that premise and then escalate.

The story began a trend at *The Onion* of the "assault of the puns" story. Every once in a rare while, *The Onion* will run another silly story that's made up of as many puns as it can fit. "Fritolaysia Cuts Off Chiplomatic Relations with Snakistan" and "Bo Obama Receives Visiting Dognitaries from Furuguay" are two notable examples.

After organizing, rewriting, and vetting stories for the whole book for months, I delegated large sections to others. Maria would be the section editor of the first third of the century, John the middle, and Robert the last. I continued to vet the headline jokes, but Maria, John, and Robert saved me a lot of work by filling out stories and getting them in pretty good shape before I saw them.

My favorite part of the book project was the writer printouts. I would print rough, unfinished pages, and then the writers would write things on these printouts and give them back to me. These pages were gold. I got to know everyone's handwriting well. Mike's precise and angular words had incredibly smart jokes about political unrest and CIA coups. John's barely discernible etchings created so many of the pithy *Onion* mottos at the tops of pages. Maria and Todd could always be counted on to improve stories by handwriting whole new paragraphs, expanding the escalation or adding new joke beats. Tim, however, was the best at joke beats. He was a joke machine. If I showed him a story and made sure he knew the take, he could write joke beats for it until you told him to stop. I loved seeing his large, childlike handwriting on the sheets. Robert would add subheadlines and tweaks to main headlines, often writing several subtle variations of each on the back of the sheet, trying to get the wording perfect and get at the heart of the joke. Carol had handwriting like Tim's, and a knack for exploring unusual angles on stories to try to find unexpected humor.

Carol helped me get the wording just right on the feature photo that we planned for the cover of the book: the famous photo of Harry Truman holding up the newspaper that erroneously said "Dewey Defeats Truman." We changed the headline to, "Other Guy Defeats What's-His-Face."

As I edited pages and filled them out, I could sometimes write whole missing stories by simply stringing together suggestions from the scrawled notes writers had made and just adding connective tissue. I could make subheadlines and photo captions from their notes. The notes also let me know when a story wasn't working. If enough people made the note "this isn't funny" or "this isn't working," I would at least know what direction not to go in, and I could usually find the right take on my own.

I sat at a giant old metal desk we'd picked up for $30 at Madison's Buy and Sell Shop. I worked in a tiny office that I shared with the graphics team, Mike and his right hand, Chad Nackers.

Mike and Chad found photos from archive services and got them through the mail. The photo rights cost us a fortune. When we couldn't get the rights, we just stole the photos, hoping that by Photoshopping them enough, we would be in "fair use" territory.

One understandable reason Pete didn't want to pay us extra for the book was that we were spending more money to produce the book than the publisher had paid us. The project was a money loser before it was even published.

There were so many stories and so many pages to pour over, the work felt insurmountable at times. I was working the writers ragged. Robert focused on the newspaper and website while I largely pulled back from even an oversight role. *The Onion* was a well-oiled machine pumping out some of the best news satire in this period than it ever had before. This was *The Onion's* golden age.

The book, renamed *Our Dumb Century*, remained my focus all day, every day, for well over a year. I came in early and worked until I couldn't stay awake, rewriting stories, cobbling writers' jokes together or writing my own when none of the notes bore fruit. It was solitary work—perfect for my reclusive nature. But the notes always improved my own writing because it was like all the writers were there with me, on paper, and we were putting our heads together, thinking as one. My face was buried in papers at my corner desk as the writing staff brainstormed with me through their scribbles.

My edited pages circulated around the entire writing staff once again for more punch-up. This was an added layer to the process—a luxury we didn't often have on the weekly paper. But since this was our book, we wanted it to be as perfect as we could make it. This was our *Citizen Kane*.

Making the pages look accurate to their time period fell to our design staff. We were lucky to have Scott Templeton working for us. He knew about fonts, what years certain fonts were created, and in which eras newspapers tended to use them. So, he made sure the fonts were authentic. Andrew Welyczko laid out pages, as did Scott. Jack Szwergold did as well. Jack also had a hand in joke writing and illustration for the book. Mike, Maria and I did all the other art, matching our styles with the look and feel of the time. Except for Jack, we had all been cartoonists for *The Daily Cardinal*.

The next step in the process was to age the older pages, which was done simply by crumpling the printouts and re-scanning them.

After the pages were finished, the mix of the beautiful design, big headline jokes, and full articles began to excite people within the company. We knew we were working on something special. There was an electric feeling around the office that *The Onion* really could be bursting with something unexpectedly wonderful, something that might make people take notice of us in a big way. Our manager, David Miner, summed it up later when he said the book was "so much better than it had to be."

Still more punch-up was done. It seemed everyone on staff was a perfectionist, myself included. And unlike with the newspaper, where the weekly printing deadline forced us to wash our hands of it and release it at a certain point, *Our Dumb Century* could be poured over and perfected. This was a blessing and a curse. If left to our own devices, we might still be working on it today.

I finally put a stop to it and sent what we had to our editor at Hyperion, and waited.

The audiobook was next. I wanted it to be an elaborate radio mockumentary of the twentieth century. I corralled performers from the Radio Pirates as well as Todd Hanson and a wonderful voice actor named Kristina Stadler. Tim Harrod also performed, adapted the book into radio script format, and spun out a lot more joke beats for some of the material. I performed, mixed, and directed the project.

I was tremendously proud of the audiobook. It was a worthy audio equivalent of the book, albeit abridged. The historical recordings sounded authentic, and the humor translated beautifully.

Then something strange happened. A few weeks after turning in the manuscript, I received a full, unbound copy of it back in the mail from Hyperion. A cover letter explained that the publisher's legal staff had reviewed the book and suggested some changes, which were reflected in the manuscript as large X's written with a thick black marker on virtually every story on every page. Any story having to do with race, sex, or politics was X-ed out. And I don't mean objectionable lines or phrases or even headlines. I mean whole stories summarily crossed out. A year and a half of our lives, working 12-hour days with no vacation, crossed out by some Disney lawyer who didn't understand that a history of the United States couldn't possibly be told without race, sex, or politics.

I called Daniel and told him I wouldn't be dealing with Hyperion anymore. We needed to take this book somewhere else. Daniel sent the manuscript to other publishers and a bidding war ensued. He landed us at Three Rivers Press, an imprint of Random House, for a $450,000 advance.

What's more, we didn't have to pay Disney back the $100,000 they'd paid us. We had held up our end of the deal—we delivered a book as promised (albeit way past the deadline).

Three Rivers was grateful to have the book, and our new editor, Steve Ross, understood its potential. His legal department only had a handful of minor changes to suggest. I capitulated on most of them. In all cases, I agreed to scrap a joke or story only if I thought it could be funnier. If something was funny, I fought for it, and believed if someone threatened to sue us over anything, only good publicity would result. Random House's lawyers wanted us to cut our Oprah story (Oprah was like a combined God, Devil, and Thanos of the publishing industry at the time), but I argued that the piece was harmless ("Oprah Secedes from U.S., Forms Independent Nation of Cheesecake-Eating Housewives").

Sadly, none of the writers nor I would see any money from this new advance either. And to this day, *Our Dumb Century* has earned out its advance and *The Onion* receives a check for thousands of dollars a year from sales of the book, and the writers don't get a penny of it.

In interviews, when people would ask Todd how he felt about the financial success of *The Onion*, he would say with a straight face, "Some savvy business people are making a lot of money from *The Onion*, and we writers just want to say, whoever and wherever these people are, we're very proud of them."

When the book won the Thurber Prize for American Humor that year (we hadn't even submitted it for the award; the Thurber House simply recognized it as deserving, and awarded it to us anyway), I insisted their representative send the $5,000 check to me personally, not *The Onion*, and I divvied up an equal share to everyone who had worked on the book.

The book came out April 1, 1999, and was an immediate hit, debuting at number one overall on Amazon, and number one on the *New York Times* bestseller list. Because of its success, I appeared on several shows, *Late Night with Conan O'Brien* and *Fresh Air with Terry*

Gross—two of my favorites—among them. The reviews coming back both in America and the UK, where the book was simultaneously released, were glowing. The Brits tipped their hats, incredulous that someone in America had done satire better than them.

I felt like I was on top of the world. I took a vacation to Hawaii for two weeks by myself. It was my first vacation in several years. I rented a jeep and drove around the Big Island, slept on Punaluʻu Beach and swam with the giant turtles there.

A few months later, I left *The Onion*, feeling like I had achieved everything I had ever imagined I could with it. I didn't realize at the time how wrong I was.

16
9/11

The Onion had labored in relative obscurity in Madison, Wisconsin, for over ten years, but with the success of our book and website in the mid and late 90s, we were getting a lot more national media attention.

One thing bothered me about all the coverage: whenever someone would write about us or talk about us on TV or radio, they always had to point out that *The Onion* was from Madison, Wisconsin. This needled me. It made *The Onion* sound like some kind of local phenomenon. The adjective was constant: "The Madison, Wisconsin-based humor publication, *The Onion*." That's how the national media always referred to us. It made us sound small-time.

From a brand perspective it wasn't good for *The Onion*. For us to live out the most heightened version of our brand, we needed to be big-time. We needed to be national. We needed to be in New York.

I knew if we moved to New York, *The Onion* would be perceived as a national publication, not a local college paper from Madison, Wisconsin. No one would ever call it "The New York, New York-based humor publication, *The Onion*." It would just be "*The Onion*," and that unpleasant adjective "Madison, Wisconsin-based" would be deleted from the conversation.

That's what I wanted.

Pete didn't think we could afford the move, and he would have to approve the expenditure, per our agreement. I lobbied hard for it. I got the writing staff riled up about it. But he wouldn't relent. This effort, as well as other frustrations about writer pay and simply my feeling that I had done all I could for *The Onion* by then, led me to resign as editor-in-chief in 2000. I remained part-owner, but packed up and moved to Boston just to be somewhere completely different for a while.

The writers who remained continued to badger Pete on the issue and eventually he threw up his hands, saying it was a foolhardy move that could cripple *The Onion* financially. He felt like he didn't have much of a choice if he wanted to hold onto the remaining writing staff who had made *The Onion* what it was.

So, the staff moved to an expensive Manhattan office in West Chelsea, no better or worse than its office in Madison, although the new office at least had a door buzzer. In total, tens of thousands of dollars was spent to make the move to New York happen, and hundreds of thousands more would be spent to keep everyone there for years to come.

One of the first articles I read about *The Onion* shortly after the move was from *The Daily Telegraph*, the British newspaper. To my great relief, they just called it *"The Onion."* The compound-adjective about Madison was gone, and I knew it would never return. Cutting that word was probably the single most expensive copyedit in history.

In the early years of *The Onion* there wasn't a lot of highbrow satire, and rarely a cogent point about society or any other subtext. It was the University of Wisconsin Chancellor naked. It was "Heenan for President," "Special Spring Planting Issue," and "Run for Your Lives!" Perhaps the most prescient story in *The Onion* in its first year was "Dead Guy Found," which at least showed how *The Onion* would one day skewer the tropes of journalism. But even that idea was played mostly for laughs without much satire. The picture featured a large snow pile with a guy's legs sticking out of it. The modern *Onion* would have used more verisimilitude, showing police milling about a crime scene, shot from behind the police tape, to play it straight and make it look more believable.

In the ten years we'd spent refining our voice, we discovered that a more satirical edge, presented in a funny way, had broader appeal, and was therefore more popular than the more overtly shocking or juvenile humor of our early days. Stories like "Microsoft Patents Ones, Zeroes," "U.S. Unenjoyment Rate at All-Time High," and "Area Man Busts His Ass All Day, and for What?" were intelligent but also popular.

This kind of news satire represented *The Onion* as its most outrageous self, taking the idea of news parody to its pinnacle: news-based humor that poked fun not just at journalism, but at politics, culture, and the human condition.

Our Dumb Century brought our satire to a new level. It taught us that we could be subtle and have something to say not only about current events but also about how those events are perceived by history. At the same time, we could hit people over the head with broad humor: "FDR: 'The Only Thing We Have to Fear Is a Crippling, Decade-Long Depression,'" "Holy Shit: Man Walks on Fucking Moon," and "New President [Clinton] Feels Nation's Pain, Breasts."

Our Dumb Century taught us that the formula *Comedy = Tragedy + Time* was inaccurate. Our Titanic headline from 1912 ("World's Largest Metaphor Hits Iceberg") wasn't too soon. Everyone involved with that particular catastrophe was long gone. We could say anything we wanted about it. But with something more current, like the Alfred P. Murrah Federal Building bombing in 1995, survivors were still traumatized. We wondered why treatment of this topic should be any different within pages of the same book.

Our Oklahoma City bombing story, looked at one way, was probably the most insensitive and wrong-headed story in *Our Dumb Cen-*

tury. It made fun of the religious beliefs of the victims of the trage-dy ("Grieving Families of Oklahoma City Bombing Victims Turn to Angels").

Looked at in a different way, it could be perceived as neutral, that we understood people's desire to believe in angels in a time of trag-edy. This harkened back to a story we'd published in the newspaper and website about JonBenet Ramsey, the six-year-old beauty pageant contestant who was murdered in 1996. It was an *Onion* editorial, sup-posedly written by her, titled "Don't Feel Sad, I'm in Heaven Now, Singing with the Pretty Angels." It was a kind story, more sad and understanding than funny.

In either case, whereas even an insensitive Oklahoma City story put out by *The Onion* newspaper or website would have drawn the ire of readers, we never heard a peep about our story in the book. It was contextualized as a book of history, so time had been removed from the equation, and people weren't offended.

The Onion's writers were exploring new ways to approach our work, tackling current events using different emotions beyond just humor.

In *The Onion*'s first 15 years, we hardly ever wrote about current events in the news cycle. Our weeks-long lead-time for production made it impossible to respond in a relevant way to breaking news. We simply made up fake stories about newsy subjects. We could only sat-irize stories that spanned weeks, like the War in Iraq or the undecided Bush–Gore election of 2000. When a major news event happened, like when O.J. Simpson was found not guilty, *The Onion* couldn't jump on it in a timely manner like, say, a late-night talk show could. This inability to react masked a deeper insecurity. I knew making fun of a story currently making history was a bigger responsibility than mere made-up news. We would have to make sure it wasn't too soon, and we would have to choose our targets carefully, making sure not to punch down. Maybe I didn't think we were ready for that kind of satire.

But we were learning. Another thing we began to understand was the healing power of laughter.

Onion writers were becoming comfortable with the concept of the "line" that shouldn't be crossed. They had already learned the lessons of whom to attack and why, but now they were beginning to uncover a deeper truth about satire they had already discovered in their personal journeys, but perhaps not yet on the page: satire is a tool we can use to help other people—not just ourselves—process terrible things in the world.

The Onion's 9/11 issue was remarkable for not only responding to a news event (albeit two weeks later), but for devoting an entire issue to that single event. The only other time *The Onion* had done a one-event edition was the undecided election roughly a year earlier, with stories like "Clinton Declares Self President for Life" and "Serbia Deploys Peacekeeping Forces to U.S."

But Bush v. Gore wasn't a national tragedy on the scale of 9/11.

On the evening of September 10, the *Onion* staff celebrated its move to New York with a big "Welcome to New York" bash. The band They Might Be Giants performed, and drinks and laughs were had by all in attendance.

The next morning, after the planes struck the twin towers, the staff didn't come to work. They held off publishing their first New York print edition of *The Onion*, instead taking an unplanned two-week break from publication, which was unheard-of for *The Onion*.

After the attacks, the entire country was scared and shocked. New York city was heartbroken. Pundits proclaimed the end of satire, the end of irony, and even the end of comedy itself. Could we ever laugh again? people wondered.

When the staff of *The Onion* finally convened, about a week after the attacks, they began discussing the next issue. Any stories about anything other than the attacks seemed to minimize what everyone in the country was going through. 9/11 was the only thing anyone was thinking about. It needed to be written about.

So, they started their process, brainstorming hundreds of headlines to select the best ones. They used their gut instinct, honed from years writing news satire and the intense process of writing news-parody responses to national tragedies in *Our Dumb Century*. They knew they needed to create headlines that felt right, that seemed to capture the mood, not with hilarity, but with an appropriate level of understanding that would help people deal with the tragedy.

A story I sent in from Boston, about George W. Bush blasting the Psychic Friends Network for failing to predict the attacks, was rejected. A headline from Tim Harrod, "America Stronger Than Ever, Say Quadragon Officials" was also passed on. These were deemed off-target, trying too hard to be funny, or making fun of the wrong things.

The headlines had to be genuine, not cute or clever. And they had to provide some kind of release. At this time, it was a knowing sense of shared loss that would connect people, not gut-busting jokes.

Headlines that worked were "Hijackers Surprised to Find Selves in Hell," which was a wonderfully cathartic piece in which the terrorists who flew the planes into the World Trade Center were described being horribly tortured in a gruesome display of cartoonish physical comedy. "Not Knowing What Else to Do, Woman Bakes American Flag Cake," was a sublime slice of life from Carol. The banner of the news for that issue, "Holy Fucking Shit: Attack on America" was an escalation of the "Holy Shit" moon-landing story from *Our Dumb Century*.

This type of profanity-based catharsis humor was a precursor to some of *The Onion*'s coverage of school shootings in the years that followed. Sometimes a well-meaning swear or two is all that can be said. Sometimes satirists have to set aside the wackier tools in the toolbox and simply try to connect with people on a human level and say what everyone is thinking.

The Onion's 9/11 issue was a heartfelt literary response to an American tragedy. It was written and edited by a thoughtful group of satirists who had just moved to the big city from Madison, Wisconsin, who never expected to be thrust into a national conversation about a violent attack that resulted in the deaths of 3,000 people. Most readers who saw the issue, myself included, felt a sense of relief, a return to normalcy, like it was okay to laugh again after being so deeply stunned and hurt.

In a way, it's exactly the position *The Onion* had asked to be thrust into. The entire staff wanted to move to New York. We all wanted to be in the big leagues.

The 9/11 issue was on the short list for a Pulitzer that year. Readership doubled. Many people still remember the issue as *The Onion's* finest hour. In its small way, it contributed to the nation's healing process, showing us all that humor is indeed an important coping mechanism in times of tragedy.

And for *The Onion* itself, the 9/11 issue further cemented the publication's identity as a place not just for new-parody, but a place where humor could be elevated to something that humanity actually needs, a place to go for a little bit of the cleansing power of a good laugh after a time of sorrow, just as it has always been for those of us who wrote for it.

After 9/11, perhaps incidentally, I never again felt like *The Onion* was one issue away from going out of business. It felt like it had dug in its heels, and found a permanent place in American culture.

17
CEASE AND SUCCESS

In the 1992 NBA finals, game one, Michael Jordan felt like he couldn't miss. He made 35 points in the first half, 3-pointer after 3-pointer, breaking records and shocking observers. It's called "the shrug game" because Jordan at one point looked at the camera and shrugged. He was in flow state, making 3-pointers like they were free throws.

Jordan's shrug is the most succinct definition of success I've ever seen. When it's happening, it feels like an out-of-body experience, like you're taking a ride on a rocket ship that you don't control.

The Onion is the most well-known success I've been fortunate enough to be involved with. "Jim's Journal" is a distant second. Another is a book I wrote a long time ago that remained in print for years and had a big impact on a lot of people. It was a parody of a self-help book called *You Are Worthless*. I wrote the book when I was in a dark place. My wife had just left me and an independent film I'd made and invested all my money in had fallen apart and the production was scuttled after the film was only half shot.

Having lost the only two pillars of emotional support I had (relationship and career), to say nothing of being broke, I felt like the rug had been pulled from under me. I was emotionally fragile because I had only just learned to interact with people normally. I was chronologically an adult, but emotionally I was probably about six years old. I had lived my life as little more than a comedy-producing robot. My feelings were raw. I dealt with this experience in the only way I knew how: by writing jokes. I let out all my darkest, most dispiriting, least helpful thoughts. They came out as one-liners:

You are good for nothing.

Tomorrow is going to be even worse than today.

Love is a deep, dark chasm of pain and loss.

You are not very good in bed.

If you take a big risk and follow your dreams, chances are you're going to fall flat on your face. On the upside, everyone around you will get a good laugh.

Maybe you should binge on ice cream.

They piled up. I started sorting them in categories: "Your Worthless Self," "Your Good-for-Nothing Friends," "Your Miserable Job," and "Life—What's the Use?"

Pretty soon, I realized I had a book. I drew little illustrations to go along with some of the sayings and sold the book to Andrews McMeel, the publisher who handled all my "Jim's Journal" books and who was eager to try something else with me. I was surprised they went for it. They're a family-friendly company. *You Are Worthless* was incredibly dark, with several calls for readers to commit suicide and shoot up malls, "just to see if anyone will finally notice you." Yet the people at Andrews McMeel were wonderful to me—they still are (they manage gocomics.com, which continues to distribute "Jim's Journal"). They flew me down to their headquarters in Kansas City—twice. I met all the leaders of the company and they wined and dined me. They're an absolute delight.

Another success I enjoyed was a comedy podcast I created with my high-school radio-comedy cohort Peter Hilleren.

When President George W. Bush won re-election in 2004, Peter and I began doing a weekly podcast that parodied his weekly radio address. The president's weekly radio address was a tradition since FDR's fireside chats. Obama updated it to a YouTube address. Trump discontinued it. But Bush did it the traditional way, issuing a short, audio-only message available to the public and the news media. It had its own page on the whitehouse.gov website. It was released every Saturday morning.

Peter and I decided it would be fun to spoof it. I had been working on my George W. Bush impression for a while, and it was passable, so we got together at my little Brooklyn recording studio and worked up some bits. We played off actual things George W. Bush had done in the news every week. If there was no big news, we would just make up something silly. We would each write three or four one-minute sketches, and then I would read through them in the studio. Peter engineered and directed. I would improvise a little to make it sound natural. Peter would mix it and put the intro and outro on it, and that's how we made an episode.

Peter copied the HTML from the White House website so our website would look authentic. People could listen to past episodes from our website or on iTunes, and sign up for our email list, just like with the real address.

We kept this up every week during the second term of the Bush Administration. It was a fun little project for us. The podcast, *The Weekly Radio Address*, became quite popular, often appearing in the iTunes top 15 despite the fact that we didn't promote it. It routinely ranked higher than Bush's actual weekly radio address, which was also distributed as a podcast.

The episodes were always silly. Some typical episodes: a recap of his recent veto of a stem-cell-research bill explaining he had personally adopted the stem cells and put them in microscopic cribs, a summary of his recent address to "The National Association of Coloreds," a demonstration of all the "buttons of leadership" he can press at his oval-office desk, and an episode where Dick Cheney explains that he ate the man he shot in the face because "a good hunter doesn't kill anything he doesn't eat."

The way most people found podcasts when the medium first appeared was through iTunes, and iTunes had a habit of promoting podcasts they liked in their "new & notable" section and elsewhere. They promoted ours a few times. We didn't have to pay for this promotion and often didn't even know about it. There were certain badges and other images that iTunes recommended be uploaded if creators wanted to be considered for such promotions. We simply followed the best practices and grew organically without spending any money on marketing. This was easier to do when podcasts were new and everyone on the planet didn't have their own podcast like today.

I always like to get in on the ground floor of new media. It's easier to get noticed.

A few opportunities came our way as a result of the podcast. I got hired to do George W. Bush's voice in commercials and in song parodies and skits for *Springer on the Radio* on Air America. I also got cast in one of Robert Smigel's "TV Funhouse" cartoons for *SNL*, doing Bush's voice for the episode "Torboto: the Robot that Tortures People."

Peter and I also hatched a book idea based on the podcast. We had created this comedic character of George W. Bush that we thought would be fun to flesh out in a comprehensive parody autobiography. We began developing framing ideas for the book.

Though I wasn't working at *The Onion* at the time, I occasionally consulted with the new owners, and they liked the idea of featuring *The Weekly Radio Address* podcast on the *Onion* website, much like Fox News featured the president's weekly radio address on theirs. *The*

Onion picked it up, and our iTunes ranking got a boost.

Because of the podcast's following, we had the opportunity to run ads on it, but we refused because it would have destroyed the verisimilitude of the parody—a signature Outrageous Marketing strategy: choosing brand identity over profits.

In October of that year, *The Onion* received a cease-and-desist letter from the White House Legal Affairs office claiming the presidential seal can't be used for commercial purposes or to suggest any official endorsement by the president. At the time, the White House Legal Affairs office was in the news, with staffer Harriet Miers having recently been appointed by Bush as a nominee for the Supreme Court. Her nomination failed pitifully in the face of strong bipartisan opposition. Nobody liked the idea that she was one of Bush's friends, didn't seem intellectually curious, but most importantly, had never served as a judge in any capacity.

While back working for *The Onion* by then, I immediately recognized the letter as an opportunity, and sent it to *The New York Times*. They ran a piece about the incident on the front page of their Arts section. I also sent a jokey response to the White House, saying I was surprised the president deemed it a smart move to spend taxpayer money for lawyers to send cease-and-desist letters to comedians.

The day the *New York Times* story came out, our agent scheduled meetings at several publishing houses to pitch the autobiography project. The publicity ignited a bidding war. We ended up settling on an offer with Scribner for a $250,000 advance.

The book, *Destined for Destiny: The Unauthorized Autobiography of George W. Bush,* was well-reviewed. I was exceedingly proud of it. The hardcover, especially, was beautiful. It was the first time I had published a hardcover book. In the middle of the book, we featured a section of black-and-white photos on thick glossy paper stock depicting Bush's life, as you would expect in a biography. But in our book, realistically Photoshopped into each family photo was none other than Jesus Christ.

The cover featured an original photo of Bush leaning against a rustic fence on his Crawford, Texas, ranch. The photo had been taken as part of a photoshoot for Scribner, which was the official publisher of all the Bush family biographies. Our book is the only time the photo has been used. So, in effect, the president posed just for us.

Now I've told you about my most successful endeavors. One of the principles of Outrageous Marketing is quantity to achieve quality. Accordingly, there are a lot more stories to tell about projects I've been involved with that have failed: two feature films that lost money, an animation company that couldn't get off the ground, and many others. But that's a subject for another book. Look for *Scott Dikkers' Big Book of Failures,* which I'm sure will be a big success.

18

WAIT, A PEABODY?

One of my favorite things to do after I left *The Onion* in 2000 was to pick up the paper on the street and enjoy it just like a fan. Robert Siegel was, in my opinion, the finest writer or editor *The Onion* ever produced. He was the editor then, and for the 9/11 issue. He wrote, or largely rewrote, most of the articles. He held the line on *The Onion*'s strict adherence to its brand of AP style that never winked at the audience.

Robert left in 2003, and his assistant editor, Carol Kolb, took over for just two years. She had become an excellent leader. Her staff was largely unchanged since I had been owner and editor-in-chief. In fact, the newspaper and website hadn't changed much. It adhered to the same format. The only new project it pursued in those years was *The Onion Movie*, which was still unreleased. The only new writers were Chris Karwowski, who had been a contributor since the 90s, and Peter Koechley, *The Onion*'s first intern. I hired him when we were still in Madison. He had produced an *Onion*-like publication as a senior at Madison West High School who struck me as a capable and ambitious young man. In the years I was gone, he served as a freelance *Onion* headline contributor while getting his degree from Columbia University. *The Onion*'s second intern was Aziz Ansari, but he was scarcely allowed in the writers' room. The writers were very exclusive about their club, so Aziz was relegated to being an ad-staff intern.

By 2005, Pete Haise and I had sold all our voting shares in the company to investor David Schafer. David, along with Steve Hannah, his handpicked CEO, and Steve's lieutenant, Sean Mills, met with me and asked if I had any suggestions for a new *Onion* editor. Apparently, Carol was leaving and they didn't see any clear replacement from within.

Maybe, like me, they hadn't even been introduced to Aziz.

I told them what I thought *The Onion* needed now: new blood, a younger and hungrier New York staff, new projects, maybe a new book. I also told them I didn't want *The Onion* to rest on its laurels or become like a museum, where the goal was merely to preserve some kind of *Onion* legacy. This was an unfortunate tendency among writers and editors. Because many of them hadn't seen *The Onion* go through changes in its early years, they had a different philosophy about the brand's malleableness. I felt strongly that *The Onion* needed to keep evolving to continue to find its most outrageous self.

I recommended they look at David Rees, the multi-talented writer and performer who'd made a popular comic strip, "Get Your War On," and a fake ad-agency website (joeythemidwife.com) that was one of the funniest things I'd ever seen. I thought *The Onion* could use a bold new voice like David's.

Instead, they offered the job to me.

I had mixed feelings about the offer. In the end, I realized *The Onion* is in many ways my child. I helped bring it into the world, raised it, rocked it to sleep, held its hand on the way to its first day at kindergarten, took a picture for its first prom date, and cried as I sent it off to college.

I couldn't say no. I started in June 2005.

The first thing I did was head up the writers' meetings. I wanted a direct hand in selecting each headline. I threw my weight around a lot more than I had in the early days because now I had been on the out-side, in the real world, enjoying *The Onion* like any reader, which gave me a valuable perspective and renewed confidence that I knew what *The Onion* needed. Selecting the headlines was the highest-leverage thing I could do to keep *The Onion* focused on being the most outrageous version of itself. From that foundation I wanted it to grow.

I also brought in new writers. An intern, Mike DiCenzo, seemed like a smart and funny guy, so I offered him the chance to submit a story. His story was not only good, it was polished—almost print-ready. His draft, for "Bush Vows to Eliminate U.S. Dependence on Oil by 4920," instantly raised the bar for the other writers, who were still spoiled under the previous system where poor drafts could be handed in to the editor for a significant rewriting. Chad Nackers, whom I had invited to submit jokes back in Madison, was still primarily doing graphics. I assigned him stories, and he proved to be as competent as Mike. I also hired Dan Guterman, a teenager from Canada who had been submitting jokes to *The Onion* for a while. After he visited the office for a few days and proved to be exactly the kind of lovable sad sack that made for a great satirist, *The Onion* completed a mountain of legal paperwork to get Dan a green card so he could come to New York and join the staff full-time. He was a master jokesmith with a dark sense of humor who knew how to make his work accessible to a wide audience. One of his first stories for *The Onion* was "Guy In Philosophy Class Needs to Shut the Fuck Up." Another writer I hired was Seth Reiss, who was introduced to me by Mike DiCenzo. Seth first started writing sports stories for John Krewson's new *Onion* Sports section, but he quickly found a place on the main writing staff, writing peculiarly small, relatable stories like "Law Firm to Purchase One of Those Big Leather Chairs," and "Rubber Band Needed," which harkened back to the "Pen Stolen" days of *The Onion*.

I promoted Peter Koechley to Managing Editor. He and I implemented *The Onion*'s Writing Fellowship program, a three-month opportunity for young writers to work on our staff. It was another way to find promising new talent. We invited writers from college humor publications around the country to submit their work. Our first *Onion* Fellow was Megan Ganz from the University of Michigan's *Every Three Weekly*. She quickly proved to be a capable and outspoken member of the writers' room, despite the fact that she was ten years younger than everyone else, except Dan. After her fellowship was over, I immediately hired Megan to be a full-time staff writer. She wrote one of my all-time favorite pieces of writing in *The Onion*, an editorial by Dr. Seuss: "Stop Making Movies About My Books."

I brought in a steady stream of interns. Aside from helping us with administrative tasks, like organizing headline lists and taking notes at meetings, *Onion* interns made excellent writers-in-training. Their internships served as a way to learn *The Onion*'s company culture and writing system. Peter was a smart and inventive Managing Editor. Will Tracy was an intern in 2005 and went on to become *The Onion*'s editor-in-chief. Aziz Ansari was a tragic missed opportunity. He was long gone and already doing stand-up around New York before my return.

When my assistant editor, Amie Barrodale, departed, she alerted me to someone in her improv class named Joe Randazzo. I needed an assistant editor in a hurry. I didn't have time to put a new person through the thorough, years-long process of becoming an intern and then a contributor and then a staff writer. Joe worked at a fruit-basket store but was not only a funny performer and writer, he had written news for radio. I gave him a simple editing test by asking him to edit an *Onion* story that was in rough shape. He did a passable job, far better than I'd ever seen from someone who had no experience writing for *The Onion*. So, I hired him and began training him to edit and write in the *Onion* style. He became a superb editor, a great manager, and went on to be *The Onion*'s editor-in-chief for several years.

With headlines like "Kansas Outlaws Practice of Evolution," "Wrongly Imprisoned Man Won't Shut Up About It," "NASA Chief Under Fire for Personal Shuttle Use," and "Fire Truck! Fire Truck! Fire

Truck!" an editorial written by a four-year-old, I felt like *The Onion* was headed in the right direction.

We embarked on another original book project, *Our Dumb World,* a world atlas parody that further defined our brand as a (fake) trusted authority. It became a bestseller. Still, by 2006, we had no marketing budget. Our product was our marketing. Social media was blowing up around us but we weren't using it. Many of us were scarcely aware of it.

The Onion was still parodying *USA Today*. *USA Today* was a relevant news source to be parodying when *The Onion* was created in 1988. But by the mid 00s, the most relevant target was Fox News. My first thought was simply to change *The Onion* into a print version of Fox News. Sean Mills convinced me such a change would be too radical for *The Onion*, that it would confuse advertisers.

Later that year *The Colbert Report* debuted on Comedy Central, co-created and executive produced by former *Onion* editor Ben Karlin. It was an enormous hit. Ben acted where I had failed to. *The Colbert Report* was a brilliant parody of Bill O'Reilly's show on Fox, which audiences were hungry to see spoofed. *The Colbert Report* was an even closer cousin to *The Onion* than *The Daily Show*, given that Colbert, like *The Onion*, never broke character, whereas Jon Stewart winked and mugged for the camera constantly.

By 2005, the bandwidth of most people's Internet service had reached the point where podcasting had become popular. *The Onion Radio News* was consistently in the iTunes top five. Bandwidth was in fact increasing every day, and streaming video was on the horizon. The first YouTube video had been uploaded in April of that year. Netflix was only distributing physical DVDs. There was no Amazon Video. No Funny or Die. Most streaming video online was two- to three-minute clips from news network websites. There was competition and compatibility issues between Windows Media, RealPlayer, and QuickTime. Most of it took forever to download. But with speeds and compression codecs always improving, I saw an opportunity for

The Onion to step in and plant a flag in the new medium of online video.

I met with the writers to discuss ideas for videos. Mostly, the writers were nervous about doing video at all. Many of them were understandably wary after the production of the ill-fated *Onion Movie*, to say nothing of *The Comedy Castaways* or my less-than-illustrious movie career.

The *Onion* writers' room could be quite the nursing home for curmudgeons. If they couldn't do it perfectly, they didn't want to do it at all. Regardless, I assigned them the task of coming up with video ideas. The ideas were vetted and put on a short list, per our normal process, and then scripts were assigned.

Onion meetings could often be dispiriting. The meeting we held to read through these video scripts was especially dismal. The scripts were reminiscent of *The Onion Movie*. They weren't visual. They weren't newsy enough. Some included impossibly long lines of expository dialogue, impossible-to-shoot locations or effects. Most were like the bad skits that went on too long at the tail end of *SNL* during its worst seasons.

We all knew *The Onion* would have to do better. But no one was sure how. Would it even be possible to be better than we actually were?

The success of *The Daily Show* and *The Colbert Report* loomed large over *The Onion*'s effort to launch any kind of video division. People told us, "Don't even bother trying." They said Stewart and Colbert already owned fake news on TV; there was no reason for *The Onion* to get involved.

I did some R&D with a video series called "The Economic Minute." I cast Leo Allen, one of my favorite New York comedians, to play a realistic schlub in his apartment who recounted his pitiful financial situation. Joe Randazzo played his always-sleeping roommate. The *Onion*-ness of the video came from the context: the segment, shot from the character's messy apartment, featured a packed screen of chyrons showing market indices, cramming Allen into a small portion of the screen like a talking head on Bloomberg News.

It was an inauspicious beginning. Sean, Peter, and I knew we needed a bigger effort to tackle video the right way. Peter wanted me to meet someone he met at Columbia named Will Graham. Will had been a film student there, and had a competent short film under his belt. I hired him to head up the effort to build a staff to create *Onion* web videos.

The first thing I asked Will to do was his own R&D. I largely left him alone to see what he could do. He called on his small network of peers to cobble together a crew and shot a parody of an in-the-field investigative-report-type show using comic actors. It came off jokey, like a skit on a sketch show. Like "The Economic Minute," it was well below the quality standard *The Onion* needed to exceed.

Meeting that standard was a tall order. *The Onion* had a reputation now. We had won the Thurber prize. The 9/11 issue was momentous. We had millions of fans who expected great things from us. A new web-video product from *The Onion* would not only have to live up to our best printed material, it would also have to justify existing in the same sphere as *The Daily Show* and *The Colbert Report*, which dominated satirical comedy on TV.

We scrapped R&D. Will and I worked closely to embark on applying the *Onion* system to creating video. We used quantity to find quality at every stage of the process. Will cast a wide net and compiled a huge staff of writers, drawn from people he knew at Columbia, people recruited from the UCB Theater, and people who responded to open job listings. We brought Carol back to be the head writer. With hundreds of suggestions from the new staff, we came up with shows like *In The Know*, a Sunday morning newsmaker interview program, clips from O-span, a parody of C-span, and *Today Now*, a network morning show. We devised an umbrella conceit for all the videos: a domineering network spanning the globe made up of hundreds of channels. We hyperbolized *The Onion* in a fictional universe and made it not only impossibly big, but formidable and scary—a virtual assault of news. It would be called "Onion News Network." A Fox News parody was taking shape. The *Onion* brand was sharpening to become more outrageous.

Will was an unassuming guy. He had a goofy, self-effacing demeanor. He was a little chubby, balding, and had one of the weakest handshakes I'd ever felt. But he was genuine, nice, and a joy to collaborate with. He was an incredibly hard worker and one of the most impressive managers of people I had ever seen in action. He hired great talent, many of whom went on to illustrious careers in comedy. One of our interns, Beth Newell, would one day found Reductress. com. Chris Gethard would become a comedy celebrity and author. A locations coordinator named Chris Kelly was promoted to writer, then director. He later became the head writer of *SNL*, largely responsible for one of its best runs in years.

The old guard in the *Onion* writers' room watched with a mix of dread and fascination as legions of young employees pushed into every square foot of *Onion* headquarters, clearly working longer hours, and with more passion, than anyone else in the company.

Before Will was hired at *The Onion*, our new office in SoHo had a ping-pong table that people sometimes played on. After Will, the ping-pong table was ringed with more than a half-dozen new staffers in casting, locations, costumes, and production, with piles of papers and manila folders stacked on top of it. The ad reps' wing of the office was overflowing with video staff and new file cabinets filled with actor headshots and resumés. Every corner of the office was made into a makeshift workspace. Plants were removed from walls to make room for desks. Every corner became a new station. A whole department was housed in the small hallway where we kept the trash and recycling. Despite the smell, this "trash hall team" was often the first to arrive and the last to leave.

I was stupefied by Will's ability to get his new staff worked up to achieve great things for us. To get some insight into how he did what he did, I asked Carol how she liked working for him.

"Will is the best boss in the world," she said, unironically.

Will had an unreal degree of Ken Artis's "influence without power." We were planning a video that required what's called an "actuality," an on-camera reaction to a news story, from Bill Clinton. I waved that off, expressing to Will that we could never get Bill Clinton. Will said he would try. Just a day or two later, Will told me, "Bill is into it."

I was too stunned to ask him how he had gotten in touch with Bill Clinton's people to get an answer so quickly.

I took Peter aside.

"Peter, this Will Graham—who is he? Is he really just a kid fresh out of college?"

Peter shrugged like Michael Jordan.

We continued to sit back and watch Will spin his magic.

Will had very little experience producing comedy. I taught him how to escalate a comedy sketch, which is the structure the videos needed. He was a quick study. Just as with the headlines in *The Onion*, I was sure to approve or veto every show idea, every individual video episode, and every line, getting Will up to speed on my criteria for selection winners. Will's team produced volumes of ideas, and the ideas got better after I gave Will notes about what was working and what wasn't. We then set Carol and her team of writers on the right path— the right take—for each script. We axed scripts that weren't working. Scripts that were working were written with several options ("alts") for each line of dialog so that if one line didn't work in shooting or editing we would have additional lines at the ready to replace it.

Production began on the videos, with me directing the first few in order to set the tone. Will was a quick study there, too, and began directing immediately.

Will developed another show that I didn't think would be possible. We wrote scripts for it, and I knew what it needed to be, but I didn't think we could afford to shoot it or pull it off tonally. Will proved me wrong. He put together the elements necessary to create videos parodying the breaking-news desk pieces of real news networks with anchors and a large newsroom behind them. With the help of a brilliant graphics team lead by JJ Shebesta, we now had videos that looked like they had been shot on a real news set. They were all virtual. We didn't have a boom-arm, but JJ figured out a way to replicate boom-arm shots—the kind that sweep into the anchor's close-up at the beginning of a segment. We suddenly had million-dollar newsroom clips that we produced for no more than a few thousand dollars.

Though this budget may seem thrifty, spending sometimes as much as $25,000 for each three-minute video clip on *The Onion* was madness. David invested over a million dollars in the effort. There was no immediate return. In those days, we'd be lucky to sell a $500 ad on a web video. At best, *The Onion* had been a break-even company before. Now it was hemorrhaging money. It would be many years before we developed a more sustainable business model.

But we were building goodwill. We were building a fan base. Some of us knew that was more valuable than short-term profits.

After the videos were shot, I oversaw the editing, working directly with our editors, J.J. Adler and Benjamin Moses Smith, to make the timing as authentically newsy as possible.

Many tricks were used to make the videos seem different from other comedy. I wanted ONN videos to feel like real news, not like comedy skits. Mimicking the target of the parody as closely as possible always makes it funnier.

One trick was to write the punchlines in the middle of sentences and then cut the rest of the sentence in post. We found that when actors read comedy, they instinctively punched the punchlines, even if you directed them not to. They couldn't hide the fact that they knew it was supposed to be funny. This destroyed verisimilitude, revealing that it was a performance and not real news. By adding extra lines that we knew we would cut out, the actors deemphasized the punchlines, and it registered as more off-the-cuff. In real news clips, people are often cut off in actualities, so this heightened verisimilitude. This trick stemmed from Mark Twain's advice: "The humorous story is told gravely; the teller does his best to conceal the fact that he even dimly suspects that there is anything funny about it."

Another trick we used was hiring non-actors. They're always more natural. Some of our actors were homeless or mentally ill. Casting homeless people I found outside was something I liked to do in casting my movies. Some of the most fascinating characters can be found living on the streets.

Another trick was improvising lines as much as possible. Giving actors questions they could answer on camera always resulted in more realistic actualities than feeding them pre-written lines.

All these tricks worked together to create truly believable actualities for ONN. In one video, "Use of 'N-Word' May End Porn Star's Career," we found sketchy-looking people on the street and asked them what they thought of this fake story. They pretended they knew about it and commented with genuine opinions. It was pure comedy, and better acting than you could get from Meryl Streep.

Many of the anchors we hired had real news anchor experience. It always bothered me in movies when they hired actors to play news anchors. Actors don't sound like news anchors. News anchors do.

Some of the early ONN videos showed promise: "Zoo Panda Demands Abortion"; "Ninja Parade Slips by Town Unnoticed"; and "New Wearable Feedbags Let Americans Eat More, Move Less." The O-Span video of Rep. Benjamin Sinclair (R-Ohio) introducing the Ocular Penetration Restriction Act of 2007 to end the epidemic of skull-fucking was particularly inspired.

In its stride, some of the best ONN videos were "Sony Releases Stupid Piece of Shit That Doesn't Fucking Work," "Tired of Traffic? New DOT Report Urges Drivers: 'Honk,'" and "Breaking News: Some Bullshit Happening Somewhere." "Missing Girl Probably Raped" excoriated the mainstream news coverage of missing girls. The lunacy of *In The Know* shined in panel discussions like "Are Our Children Learning Enough About Whales?" and "Is the Government Spying on Schizophrenics Enough?" One of the best clips of *Today Now*, which always brilliantly satirized the saccharin inanity of morning network TV, was "Child Bankrupts Make-A-Wish Foundation Wishing for Unlimited Wishes."

Will and I held a screening for the *Onion* newspaper writers, showing a handful of the first videos we'd made before they were finalized. The writers were no less skeptical than they were at the start, expressing their grave concern about the negative fallout if we released the videos.

I believed the videos were good. I felt like they were hitting the standard we needed them to hit.

After they were released with very little fanfare and no paid promotion (only ads in *The Onion*), the feedback started coming in. The videos were shared organically, routinely getting over a million views every week. YouTube comments were effusively positive. I received congratulatory calls from colleagues at *The Daily Show* and elsewhere asking me how we got our actors to seem so real.

TV agents approached us immediately with offers to sell a TV version of ONN. Agents had been eager to represent me and *The Onion* in the past, but I had never seen agents salivate like this.

In the early years, we used to joke in deadheads about *The Onion* being the recipient of prestigious journalism awards. Never in my most fevered dreams did I think *The Onion* would actually win one of those awards one day. But in a delightful and unexpected twist, the ONN web videos won the 2008 Peabody Award. The Grady College of Journalism and Mass Communication at the University of Georgia, which gives out the Peabody, said this:

> News parody is nothing new in electronic media. The irreverent "Weekend Update" has been a staple of *Saturday Night Live* since its debut in 1975, and mock news is the lifeblood of Jon Stewart and Stephen Colbert's Comedy Central shows. But only Onion News Network, a web offshoot of the satirical

tabloid *The Onion*, does fake news—specifically, fake cable news—so deftly that viewers may find themselves doing a double take. With anchors and sets and overblown graphics that could easily be CNN's or Fox News Channel's, ONN's deadpan reports inform us that Diebold, the controversial voting machine manufacturer, has accidentally leaked the 2008 election results two months early and that presidential candidate John McCain has pledged to cut $50 million from the federal budget by eliminating the Secret Service and defending himself with his bare fists. The jokes are sustained with realistic interviews and shrewdly edited sound bites from real newsmakers. For providing ersatz news that has a worrisome ring of truth, Onion News Network receives a Peabody Award.

At the ceremony, NBC News anchor Brian Williams said as he presented the statuette to Will, "The next Peabody goes to the most venerated, the most prestigious network . . ." He was, of course, joking.

In more fitting irony, Williams would be suspended by NBC a few years later for making up some fake news of his own.

19

MAYBE WE SHOULD TRY SOCIAL MEDIA

By 2012 *The Onion* had millions of followers on Facebook, Twitter, and YouTube. People would often ask me, "What's the secret of *The Onion*'s social media success?"

I had to laugh.

The Onion blundered into social media late in the game. While everyone else was already building followings on Facebook and Twitter, we were barely using the Internet; we were still focused on our print newspaper. Peter Koechley, who understood the Internet (he would go on to found Upworthy), encouraged us to get with the times.

When I left *The Onion* (again) in 2008, it was only just starting to become a digital company. The videos had been a success, and we started to list our "most emailed" stories on the homepage of our website (this started an unofficial competition among the writers to see who could get in the number-one spot). The only major advancement we'd made to cater to our digital audience was to release a new story or feature every day or two throughout the week instead of dumping the entire week's print issue online on the same day it hit newsstands, which is how we'd been doing it for years.

Until as late as 2012, print was *The Onion*'s primary model. We had print editions in Chicago, DC, Austin, Philadelphia, and New York City, as well as the smaller Midwestern cities where we'd started franchising in the early 90s. Our weekly production schedule was still print-based. We talked about our "front page," and "above the fold" material. Our lead time for any given story was over two weeks. We would approve the headline on Monday, assign the story on Tuesday, go over the draft on Thursday, edit it over the weekend, complete the graphics and proof it the following week, and release it on newsprint three Thursdays later. All the while, our online audience was outpacing our print audience at an exponential rate.

The Onion had built a large fan base of devoted readers. They bought our books, read our website and picked up our newspaper. I figured, what did we need with social media marketing?

The problem was that social media was getting ahead of us. While *The Onion* was inching along, publishing stories three weeks after our writers thought of them, the rest of the online world was getting used to reading jokes about current events as soon as they occurred, with topics lighting up Facebook and trending on Twitter. People would say, "I can't wait to see what *The Onion's* take will be on [whatever big 24-hour-news-cycle story everybody's talking about today]!" What they didn't realize is that *Onion* stories weren't based on current events like on *The Daily Show*. They were just "fake news" made up weeks earlier.

We hired Baratunde to show us how to use social media. He tried to impart how it could help us reach a wider audience online. We got on YouTube when we started doing *ONN*. Eventually we got on Instagram. But none of us, except Baratunde and Peter, knew how to use social media, and we were barely using it to do any marketing. When we released *Our Dumb World*, we mentioned it in our social media and on ads in *The Onion*. When we debuted *ONN* videos we did the same. Eventually we started posting our headlines there, encouraging people to go to theonion.com to read the full story.

Baratunde at least got us in the game, but I started to feel like *The*

Onion was being left behind in a broader sense. It would take a bigger change to get *The Onion* out in front of social media instead of chasing after it like the clueless, old, slow brand we had become.

This bigger change would have to wait until I left *The Onion* again and then came back four years later.

During those four years, on occasion, the capable *Onion* staff I'd left behind would tackle big news events. When Obama was elected in 2008, *The Onion*'s front page announced "Black Man Given Nation's Worst Job." On Saturday April 5, 2008, a news event happened that would cause *The Onion* for the first time ever to stop the presses—literally—and make a change to its front page. A skybox headline we'd been saving for years needed to be added after news of Charlton Heston's death. The headline: "Charlton Heston's Gun Taken from His Cold, Dead Hands."

An exception to our glacial schedule was "American Voices" (formerly "What Do You Think?"). This feature was compiled the weekend prior to printing so that our "people on the street" could express opinions on relevant subjects. This feature was easier to produce closer to the print deadline because it didn't require the in-depth vetting, review, rewriting or graphics of a full story.

It wasn't until 2012, when I had returned to *The Onion* once again, that we finally decided it was time to move to a digital production schedule instead of a print one. Too many of our top-viewed stories (we didn't measure "most emailed" anymore) were stories about a current event in the news. This, we learned, was a critical factor in a headline's shareability online. *The Onion* would now respond to events in the news cycle. Editor Will Tracy and head writer Seth Reiss, along with interim Managing Editor Kyle Ryan, put this change into effect, upending years of ossified *Onion* scheduling habits. Soon, daily meetings were held to assess stories and churn them out within the 24-hour news cycle.

After several years of people thinking *The Onion* responded to events in the news cycle, which it didn't, we finally stepped into that space online and claimed it. Fans had apparently been waiting patiently for us to start utilizing social media to be more relevant. Because when we did, they piled on. As soon as we converted to a digitally focused schedule and began making jokes about real stories in the news, our readership nearly doubled in the first two months and then kept growing.

This change was a double-edged sword. The stories were viewed and shared more, but they had less value in *The Onion*'s archive. Most of the other stories in our archive were more or less evergreen. They didn't require specific knowledge of any story in the news. Unfortunate stories like "George Zimmerman Wins Florida State Lottery," "Man with Widely Circulated Penis Pictures Not the Most Humiliated Person at Podium," and "Headline About So-Called Lobsterman Extremely Misleading" were funny at the time, but in order to understand them now, readers have to be current-events trivia masterminds.

The growth in readership was worth this small sacrifice, of course. Still, to mitigate its effects, I liked to keep things open for the writers. I wanted them to write headlines about whatever they were thinking regardless of what was going on in the news. This is how we discovered so many of those odd, relatable "Area Man" stories. This is how we kept our finger on the pulse of the zeitgeist, if such a thing exists.

Sometimes headlines with a two-week lead time served us better than headlines thought up expressly in response to a current event. "One Of Those Fucking People Wins New Hampshire Primary" and "Supreme Court Overturns 'Right v. Wrong'" are good examples. The best stories could refer directly to a current event in the news yet still be evergreen.

By 2014, with *Onion* stories now nominally responding to current events, and with full-time social media manager Jordan David (Baratunde left in 2011), *The Onion* was playing the social-media game slowly and steadily, never paying to promote posts, almost never responding to fans. We were just posting new stories and other features day in and day out.

So, in total, our social media strategy, such as it was, was nothing special. We had no tricks, no secrets. We were in fact usually playing catch-up with companies that had more aggressive social-media kung fu.

Social media can be inflated with clickbait, hyperengagement, bots, promoted posts, and who knows what else. But in my estimation, nothing beats a genuine fan base. When you have that, which only comes from a brand or personality people love, a tool like social media isn't a magic bullet. It's just another way for them to find you, which is all I ever wanted for *The Onion*.

20

AN ONION AD AGENCY

The Onion faced another reality in 2012. Advertisers, our true customers, were no longer satisfied being a mere banner or display ad next to an *Onion* story. They wanted to be part of the story. Like in the questionable days of *The Lucky Strike Hour* on radio in the 1930s, advertisers were ready to be in on the fun.

In the early years of *The Onion*, writers and artists on staff were happy to help make ads for the paper. But by the 2010s, the ad staff and senior management couldn't convince the writers to reach across the editorial–business divide and allow *The Onion*'s advertisers to integrate their messages into *Onion* content.

So, they turned to me, the person who'd led the *Onion* staff to accomplish so many of its biggest successes.

I can't speak too much to the creation of Onion Labs, the in-house advertising agency that was born out of this effort, except to say I was indeed involved in its development and that I disliked every minute of it.

When I returned to *The Onion* in 2012, my intention was to help keep the brand on the right course after a serious internal struggle that tore *The Onion* apart and nearly destroyed it (more on that in the next chapter). So, despite my misgivings, I did what I knew had to be done.

The Onion was struggling. It had still not fully recovered from the crash of 2008. We had a line of credit at the bank, but apparently David was done investing the big bucks. Advertising made up more than eighty percent of our revenue. We never made enough money to sustain the company selling books or T-shirts or subscriptions. *The Onion*'s ad staff was always hustling. Digital ad sales was and is a desperate, competitive business.

If *The Onion* was to continue to sell enough advertising to pay its staff, ad sales had to be made. And with advertisers demanding to move into content, I knew our editorial would need to do something akin to the days of Tim and Chris, when we pretended to glorify advertisers. We needed to either go back to playacting the role of corrupt corporate media titan who only served the interests of big money and not our readers, or come up with some other funny way to make advertisers happy.

My job was to convince *Onion* writers to come up with jokes to respond to RFPs ("requests for proposals") from advertisers. I met with Will Tracy repeatedly, and the entire staff on occasion, explaining to them that *The Onion*'s future depended on their open-mindedness about this issue.

Times had changed. In the late 80s, the Gen-X tenet was that doing commercials of any kind was "selling out." In those days, celebrities rarely did TV commercials. Bill Cosby was just about the only one. They did them in Japan, where they got big paydays but none of their fans back home would ever know they sold out. After Dana Carvey left *SNL* in 1993 as one of its biggest stars ever, he said with pride that even though he had been offered numerous commercials, he turned down more money than he made. But by the mid 10s, everybody who was famous was doing ads. There was no stigma anymore. In the preceding 25 years, audiences had grown to accept ads as part of their lives, as part of the entertainment culture. They thought nothing of their favorite celebrities endorsing products. Commercials had become the most entertaining part of the Super Bowl.

Still, the *Onion* writers were reluctant to write jokes for ads. They cooperated a little, and gave lip service to the importance of the work, but the task was never embraced. There was never a "C'mon, everybody—let's pitch in!" feeling like in the early days. Their reaction was prickly. They didn't even like being asked.

So, I put together a separate team, the Onion Labs writing team. These were people who had experience copywriting and doing comedy, but no experience writing for *The Onion*.

My first hope in building Onion Labs was that we'd encounter cool advertisers who wouldn't mind us making fun of them. We could do that all day. Advertisers who loved *The Onion* would always tell us they don't mind being made fun of.

"Oh, we'd love that!" they'd say. "We're cool. We get it."

So we'd generate ideas that viciously attacked their brand, and then suddenly they didn't get it. We would need to find new ways to make things work.

I knew the ol' "we love our advertisers but we hate our readers" routine might ring hollow if we were truly slipping advertising messages into the editorial content hoping no one would notice.

Tina Fey and the cast of *30 Rock* made it funny to hold up cans of Snapple while claiming to be against tarnishing the integrity of their show with product placements. We tried this irony approach at *The Onion* too, but you can only claim to be against product placement while actually doing it so many times.

My Onion Labs writers came up with a few campaigns advertisers liked. We scripted campaigns for companies like Clorox Bleach, Orbitz and Ford.

When I assigned ideas, I removed the brand whenever I could, simply reducing the needs of the RFP to the general subject matter. For Clorox, for example, I asked for jokes about laundry. This kept the writers feeling more free to personalize their ideas. I hoped it would produce genuine comedy that wasn't overtly salesy.

Finding it difficult to work with the *Onion* writers and now working successfully with the Onion Labs writers, I had further luck with the company's third writing team, the ONN writers. ONN was shuttering by 2012. *The Onion* could no longer afford their outsized budgets. Will Graham had left to develop shows for Amazon. JJ had become a director and was in charge of what used to be ONN. Another ONN staffer, Alex Blechman, was happy to chip in and wrote a lot of campaign ideas and scripts.

The Onion would only fund big-budget videos if they were sponsored. JJ wanted to make big-budget videos, so he had an incentive to deliver on RFP requests. And he was good, coming up with concepts that aligned with *The Onion*'s voice and advertisers' desires.

We worked together on *The Onion*'s 2012 election coverage, sponsored by 7-11, who was pushing politically themed drinking cups. The series was called "War for the White House." Videos opened with an awesome and terrifying motion graphic of stars from the American flag turning into futuristic Ninja throwing stars and slamming into the White House. One of the videos in this series, about a "Shrieking White-Hot Sphere Of Pure Rage" that had become an early GOP frontrunner for 2016, was cited years later as having predicted the rise of Trump.

When I left *The Onion* for good in 2014, experienced and energetic marketing people got hired to run Onion Labs. It generates most of *The Onion*'s revenue today. They've produced work for playful companies that jive with *The Onion*'s sense of humor, like Diet Dr. Pepper, GoDaddy, and Google's April Fools campaigns. They've also worked with more traditional brands like Ace Hardware, McDonald's, and Sprint.

So, why did I dislike this project so much?

I believe we all have to live our mission. We all have to find out what compels us in life, and we have to do that thing passionately. Coming up with ads is not my mission. I don't feel passionately about it. I like to create jokes and entertainment that says what I want it to say. I like to create satire, and I want it to be honest, expressing my actual opinion, not an opinion a big company pays me to express, like "please buy a 7-11 drinking cup." Satirists don't want to be in bed with advertisers; they usually prefer to viciously attack advertisers and the empty consumer culture they represent.

The *Onion* writers disliked the work for the same reason.

And why wouldn't they? The average person in the industrialized world sees 5,000 advertising messages every day. Isn't that enough? Why do ads have to be everywhere?

If you've ever been to Vermont, you know how beautiful and rustic it is, especially in the fall. With its quaint inns and wood fences, it's like a real-life J. Crew catalog. A big reason for Vermont's uncommon beauty is that the state doesn't allow billboard advertising. You may think such laws are anti-business or even anti-free speech, but go there some time. The lack of constant advertising in your face is cleansing, and deeply satisfying. The state probably makes a lot more money from wealthy tourists from New York City and Boston who come for its bucolic charm than it could ever make from putting up a few billboards.

Florida, with its seemingly endless rash of tacky billboards, could learn a lesson from Vermont.

But I know the world doesn't always work the way we want it to. While the *Onion* writers—myself included—might wish it weren't so, I realize *The Onion* is more Florida than Vermont.

21

THE END OF THE BRAND?

A ll told, I've only worked in a typical job (a salaried white-collar job in a cubicle) for about two years. For the rest of my career, I've been at my own company, an entrepreneur, the boss, or someone who worked alone as a freelancer. In all cases, I was blissfully unaware of the politics and Machiavellian bullshit that goes on in typical workplaces.

I'm sure such bullshit goes on not just in traditional jobs, but everywhere humans interact. Still, I've done my best to avoid it.

When I was the boss and owner at *The Onion*, I was always above the fray. I went through my days assuming the company wasn't a particularly political place. In retrospect, I realize that's foolish. There were probably devious political games being played under my radar, like with Kelly and Ben, for example. Whatever the case, I didn't engage in them. In fact, I always tried to treat people with respect and avoided interacting with employees on a non-professional level entirely. I had a reputation at *The Onion* for decades as the guy who never went to the company Christmas party (I made a brief showing at only one), and certainly didn't attend any other office social gatherings or fraternize with people outside the office. I loved all the writers on my staff. I respected their skills and their comedy minds but I didn't want to be their friend or family; I just wanted to make funny things with them. In my mind, *The Onion* was a collection of people organized to produce a product, to build a brand. It wasn't a place for people to hang out socially. It wasn't a place to find community.

That probably says more about my introverted tendencies than anything about my role at *The Onion*.

That said, I had a special relationship with a couple of people on the *Onion* staff. Mike Loew and I were roommates for a time. He offered to let me move in with him after I had been homeless. Todd Hanson and I have had a long friendship that I've always felt transcended office politics. We often met and talked outside the office and no subject was off limits. We were each other's confidant. I thought of Todd as the soul of *The Onion*.

Everything changed for me when Steve Hannah decided to close the New York office in 2011 and bring all the writers to Chicago, where *The Onion*'s business office had been headquartered for years.

None of the writers wanted to move. What self-respecting writer wants to move out of New York City? In fact, the writers—all of them—made a pact that they would stay together and refuse to be relocated to Chicago. They planned to find a buyer for *The Onion* and replace Steve in a corporate coup, possibly elevating Baratunde to CEO. I had actually encouraged Baratunde to pursue this role years earlier, believing him to be a smart and capable leader who would be great at the helm of Onion, Inc.

Failing this plan, their other option was to find an investor to fund a new project for them to pursue—a new brand to build—that would allow them to continue to work as a team and remain in New York.

I had had my disagreements with *Onion* management in the past, so I understood their frustration.

I called Steve to find out what was going on, on his end. He told me *The Onion* couldn't afford to have two offices, especially one in New York. He said he couldn't seem to communicate this idea to the writers. And he assured me that if they decided not to make the move, he would fire them and hire all new writers from The Second City in Chicago.

I've been associated with The Second City in Chicago for a long time now, and they're an amazing organization. But I knew the culture of *The Onion* would die if new people from The Second City were brought in to replace everybody. They wouldn't know the system for creating headlines or stories. They wouldn't know the writers' room culture. Even under our banner, such a radical change could deal a death blow to *The Onion.*

I set up a meeting with the writers in New York and went to talk to them to find out what was going, on their end. All the ONN writers, *Onion* writers and several contributors were there, probably thirty people. Joe Randazzo, the editor-in-chief, was their leader. The mood in the room was heated, almost toxic. A lot of them were angry with me for even talking to Steve. It seemed they thought I was messing up their chance to strike, sabotaging their leverage to get what they wanted.

Steve would never bow to their demands, I told them. He would never willingly step down to let them replace him. He would do the easy thing and fire everybody and hire new people from Chicago. I knew Steve well enough to know this was true. Steve was a businessman who believed it wasn't the current *Onion* writers who made *The Onion* special, it was the system and the goodwill of the brand. I had to agree.

I also told them they were fooling themselves if they thought they could all leave *The Onion* and start a new venture on their own and expect that readers of *The Onion* would follow them.

"You'll lose almost all of your fans," I told them. "It's writing under the banner of *The Onion* that readers follow, not you, or any new banner you might go off and start as a group."

They didn't seem to understand, and they certainly didn't agree. They didn't realize I'd laid the groundwork over decades to make *The*

Onion a powerful brand that could withstand a mass exodus of writers.

After a few days, I asked Joe if there was anything I could do to help. He told me he would let me know.

Meanwhile, Steve offered me my old job back, asking me to come to Chicago to make sure the closing of the New York office—which was going to happen one way or the other—went as smoothly as possible and didn't destroy the brand.

I told him I would do that if it became necessary, but I wanted to wait and hear from Joe. I laid low for a couple of weeks. Mike McAvoy, Steve's right hand man, began making overtures to some of the writers most likely to be open to a move to Chicago. When it seemed a handful of them might peel away and accept me as a boss if they did, Steve made my offer official.

The two or three years I worked as an employee in a traditional job, therefore, was 2012 through 2013 when I was employed by *The Onion*. After having sold all my interest in the company, I wasn't the king who gets to make all the decisions anymore. Steve was my boss.

Joe, like most of the other writers, refused to make the move to Chicago. So, when the New York office got packed up, he and the other writers parted ways with *The Onion*.

Over eighty percent of *The Onion*'s writing staff was gone.

Will Tracy would be the new editor, and Seth his head writer. A smattering of others, Chad Nackers, John Krewson and Jermaine Affonso among them, would also make the move.

But the writing staff didn't want me involved in editorial. They understandably wanted to make a go at it on their own. Will and Seth butted heads with me on occasion when I thought they were veering too far off course, but I mostly left them and the writers alone. My role was a figurehead.

While editorial plugged along on its own, largely holding steady for the first few months, I worked on Onion Labs, co-wrote and directed some videos, including the "Behind the Pen" series with Ward Sutton, in which I played Stan Kelly. I also attended a lot of meetings with various department heads to talk about who-knows-what.

In time a few new writers were brought on. Will and Seth passed on the culture and everyone coalesced into a good-sized team. The quality of *The Onion* was as high as it ever was. They were on a hot streak for a while, consistently publishing some great comedy, like a funny series of stories on the new royal baby that depicted him as the spawn of Satan, "Dolphin Spends Amazing Vacation Swimming With Stockbroker," and "You'll Never Work In This Town Again!" by the mayor of Detroit. The brilliant headline "'No Way To Prevent This,' Says Only Nation Where This Regularly Happens" headline first ran just after this period. It then recurred after each instance of a big mass shooting in America, deepening its satirical punch every time.

Joe Biden articles were in their prime in the mid 2010s. They depicted the then-Vice President as an overconfident rust-belt dirtbag in various shameless displays: "Biden Scores 800 Feet of Copper Wire," "Poll Workers Overhear Biden Repeating Phrase 'Banged Her' While Reading Names on Ballot," and "Biden Clenches Plastic Beer Cup in Teeth to Free Hands for Clapping." I worked with Will and Chad on an autobiography of Biden, with the bulk of the writing done by Alex Blechman. *The President of Vice* was released exclusively for the Kindle. When it debuted, Biden himself tweeted proudly about it and then Obama retweeted him.

Meanwhile, Joe and the other writers who left *The Onion* created a brand called Thing X in October 2012 with funding from Adult Swim. They produced fresh and funny videos and hilarious writing in the voice of Joe's particularly twisted madcap sense of humor. It was a delightful idea, in the vein of Eric Andre and *Tim and Eric Awesome Show, Great Job!* Sadly, ThingX.com shut down less than a year later, with the brand and some of the staff absorbed by adultswim.com, where it eventually disappeared altogether.

Things were going better at *The Onion*, but not for me. Steve wanted me in the office at 9 a.m., and Mike over-managed me. All I wanted was for them to tell me what needed to be done and then leave me alone to do it. But they kept taking me off projects. I got demoted several times and my salary kept dropping. Getting any projects off the ground was a challenge. Because of my propensity to give credit to my team instead of claiming it for myself, Steve and Mike sometimes voiced doubt that I had much of a hand in *The Onion*'s creative accomplishments. Yet other times, they praised me for all I'd done in the past.

One project I was able to pursue was in TV. *The Onion* had failed to keep a TV series going based on ONN or news parody in general, with both its IFC and Comedy Central shows cancelled (*Onion News Network* and *Onion SportsDome*, respectively). A pilot for Amazon Will had created just before I returned in 2012 (*Onion News Empire*, starring Jeffrey Tambor) wasn't picked up. I had my own feelings about why these shows didn't take off: I believed TV requires story, character, and emotion. But neither the IFC nor Comedy Central show used traditional story structure; they were just sketch shows with a cold, unemotional framing device. Will's show on Amazon was the best attempt of the three, but the story didn't work. *The Onion* brand needed to be applied to TV in a way that suited audience's expectations of the medium. It needed to involve a good story and characters audiences could fall in love with, while still being true to its brand identity.

In the aftermath of these failed shows, I was determined to create a show that would make sense as part of The Onion brand but that overtly avoided fake news. I came up with an animated sitcom called "Area Man," in which a regular Midwestern schlub went about his life, constantly beset by relatable problems. Meanwhile the show's framing device would elevate his personal problems into major news events.

We sold the idea to Comedy Central, but the pilot wasn't produced, and I was disheartened by the whole process. Mike and Steve forbade me to work with the other writers to complete the script. I snuck behind their backs to at least get some writers to read it and provide notes, but I wasn't able to put their talents to work in a more cooperative way that might have helped make it better.

In many ways the *Onion* office at that time was probably a typical corporate environment. Whatever the case, I didn't fit in. My anti-social tendencies didn't play well in middle management.

One day I saw a bunch of middle-aged white guys in polo shirts and blazers milling around the office, congregating in one of the large conference rooms. I didn't recognize any of them.

"Mike, who are all these guys?" I asked.

Mike smiled. "That's the board of directors."

"The what?" I asked.

"Our board of directors," he repeated, as if it were obvious.

"We have a board of directors?" I asked, incredulous. "What do they do?"

Mike smiled knowingly and headed into the conference room and closed the door.

It didn't escape my notice that neither I nor any editorial staffer had been invited to be on *The Onion*'s board of directors.

Since I was a student of Total Quality Management, I considered myself largely in service to my employees when I was the boss. So, I was well practiced at being of service and aiming to please. But over the months, I realized I wasn't particularly good at pleasing upper management. I respected their authority and did what they asked, but their stated philosophy was the opposite of mine. They believed in "managing up," a system where the employee manages the manager and not the other way around.

In the end I came to believe they brought me back to *The Onion* simply to assuage advertiser concerns that even though the staff had largely abandoned the company, at least Scott Dikkers, the founding editor, was here to make sure the torch of quality was being passed. Whether I was actually doing anything didn't really matter.

Advertising Age released a "Digital A-List" in 2013. They gave *The Onion* the number-one spot for managing the difficult transition to Chicago after losing so many New York staffers. "*The Onion* has not just survived, it's thrived," they declared.

As soon as the new writing staff was settled and doing consistently good work, I hastily departed.

The biggest change at *The Onion* after the move was that the age-old agreement between business and editorial originally forged by Pete and me was dead. There was no longer an equal balance. Business had all the power, and editorial had none. In that way, *The Onion* has become more like a traditional publication.

This was perhaps the price to pay for preserving the brand. I had an unpleasant experience working in Chicago with the new, more corporate Onion, Inc. After I left, other senior creative staffers also left frustrated. But I can't deny *The Onion* is making a lot more money than it ever made when I was in charge. And *The Onion*'s reputation remains strong with fans around the world. So, it's a powerful and successful brand by any measure.

In 2015 David sold a controlling interest in *The Onion* to Univision. I'm sure it was a smart move financially. David is an investor after all. But from a branding perspective it was odd. It still makes fans scratch their heads.

The ramifications of the sale have yet to be fully felt. But for now the culture of the writers' room remains intact. Current management, in the personage of CEO Mike McAvoy, has pledged to leave the writers alone, which is good.

I have every faith the brand will continue to survive and thrive, and I'll continue to look forward to being a reader like anyone else, enjoying a laugh at a good *Onion* story when it pops up in my feed.

22

WHO ELSE IS DOING IT?

The Outrageous Marketing I've been practicing at *The Onion* and in all my other creative endeavors is in my DNA. I've tried to illustrate it here the best way I know how, by telling the story of my time with *The Onion* and how my efforts helped bring the *Onion* brand millions of social media followers, critical acclaim, millions of dollars in profit, and household-name status.

Now I'm compelled to illustrate a few other examples of companies I've observed using some of the same principles: capitalizing on a leader's intense and emotional drive to connect with customers, producing a large quantity to find quality, defining and then refining a brand's personality, playing by a new set of rules, and using these instinctive strategies to build a world-class team that works tirelessly to make products so good that customers can't help but fall in love with them.

I'm going to look at five different brands from five different industries: one in entertainment, one in tech, one in manufacturing, one in food service, and one in health.

My entertainment-industry example, Disney, has been such a prevalent fixture of American culture for so long, it might surprise younger readers to know the company struggled for decades, surviving on little more than the fumes of its founder's passion.

Walt Disney loved to draw. He was a professional cartoonist, illustrator, and commercial artist as a teenager. He was let go at 19 and found work making crude cutout animation for an advertising agency. He was captivated by the new medium of hand-drawn cell animation, which was only a couple of years old at the time. After trying unsuccessfully to convince his boss to improve the animated commercials they produced, he quit and founded his own animation company, creating short films for a local Kansas City theater. Walt saw animation as a business opportunity and an exciting new way to touch audiences with his work.

His company failed, but he was obsessed. He headed to Hollywood to start a new animation company with his brother, Roy. While barely making ends meet for years producing cartoons for hire, forking over too much of the fruits of his efforts to distributors and studio bosses, Walt experimented with several different characters and themes with varying degrees of success, but always learning, always pushing quantity to discover quality. He endured labor and partnership troubles, but remained focused on his mission to create great entertainment.

One of the new characters he tried was Mickey Mouse. He refined it by inviting everyone from his staff, his family, and anyone who would listen, to chime in on how to make the character more lovable. He valued honest feedback over an ego boost. He wanted his creation to succeed on its merits. His longtime animation partner Up Iwerks drew the character, which they continued to refine over the years. Walt couldn't find a good distributor for his first Mickey Mouse films, but was always looking for new avenues to reach audiences. He immediately jumped into the new medium of talkies. "Steamboat Willie," featuring Mickey Mouse, became the first animated film with synchronized sound. Walt himself provided Mickey Mouse's voice. With sound, the film seemed to come to life as if by magic.

The money and distribution troubles worsened, culminating with the Walt Disney Studio losing Ub, Walt's cherished long-time collaborator, to the company that distributed the Mickey Mouse films. The owner thought he'd save money by cutting out Walt as the middleman.

After suffering a nervous breakdown caused by exhaustion, Walt continued to make Mickey Mouse cartoons and aggressively pushed the character in every available channel: comic books, newspaper comic strips, stuffed animals, and every type of licensed consumer product imaginable. He knew he had something special in Mickey Mouse, and was determined to make audiences fall in love with it.

The company's steady stream of short films started racking up Academy Awards. Walt was getting people's attention. Over more than ten years making films, he honed his skills as a storyteller. His dedicated team of animators had become the best in the business. He and his brother invested in new, innovative technologies and more animators. They were ready to dazzle audiences with a quantum leap in quality. By the late 30s, Walt turned his sites on a bigger target: feature films.

The culmination of the company's desperate work and hard-won expertise resulted in the spectacular technical and artistic triumph, *Snow White*. It was the number-one box-office hit of 1937, beloved by critics and audiences alike. It won Walt another Academy Award.

The company followed *Snow White* with several other critical successes: *Pinocchio, Fantasia, Dumbo,* and *Bambi,* none of which were hits on the scale of *Snow White.*

The studio's money woes continued. Producing animation was expensive. They burned through their *Snow White* profits quickly. During the war years, they produced training and propaganda films for the military to make ends meet. Walt hungered to continue building his brand in other channels. He tried his hand at live-action films and, later, nature films.

His brand was taking shape, largely an extension of his conservative personality. It was fun, wholesome, and family friendly.

In the 50s, he knew what his brand was. Like a brazen frontier explorer, he moved into the new medium of TV with *The Mickey Mouse Club, Disney's Wonderful World of Color,* and *Davy Crockett*—all breakthrough successes. He leveraged the public's growing fondness for his brand and heightened it to be the most outrageous manifestation of itself imaginable. His next project: an enclosed magic kingdom, a place that brought to life a clean, heart-warming fantasy world where children could play and have fun.

Disneyland itself was an impossibly expensive dream. Everyone, including Roy, whose belief in his brother never wavered as he hounded the bank for more loans, warned Walt his dream would bankrupt the company. It would cost millions more than anything they'd invested in before. Walt took out a personal loan against his own life insurance policy to begin work on the theme park.

Surprising everyone but Walt, the gamble paid off. After the success of Disneyland and then Disneyworld, as well as all the seeds Walt had planted in so many different mediums, The Walt Disney Company became a juggernaut, one of the most profitable and successful companies in American history.

Another entrepreneur who knew Outrageous Marketing, and had a drive on par with Walt Disney's, was Steve Jobs.

Steve was interested in electronic gadgets from an early age. He joined a computer club at school and, through that, got an internship at Hewlett-Packard. He teamed up with technical whiz Steve Wozniak to create the Apple Computer Company in 1976. They sold circuit boards and raised a little start-up money before building the prototype of an affordable personal computer, a product most Americans didn't know they needed.

A relentless promoter and charismatic dealmaker, Steve served as the cocky pitchman of not only his company but the entire personal-computing industry in the late 70s and early 80s. He played the underdog, selling computers that were hipper, cooler, and more attractive than stuffy IBM computers.

Computers at that time simply crunched data. They made punch cards. Governments and technology firms used them, but no one else did. They weren't sexy. Steve envisioned a world where artists would use computers: they'd design books, create beautiful photos, and compose synthesized music; they'd all have a computer in their studios.

The brand he was creating with Apple was the brand of tomorrow. Steve wanted to deliver the future.

After success with the Apple II and the failure of the Macintosh, he left the company. He started a new computer company, NeXT, a valuable failure that taught him a lot about how to build and market computers. He then bought Pixar, a fledgling computer animation company, from George Lucas. He hired great storytellers and left them alone to create the world's first fully computer-animated feature film, *Toy Story*, which became a timeless classic.

Through the 80s and 90s, Apple continued to improve its desktop computers, which were primarily sold to artists and desktop publishers.

After gaining enough perspective to see the company's potential to usher in the future, Steve returned to Apple. He was obsessed, and drove his teams to work just as obsessively. He created the futuristic-looking Apple Store. He launched the sleek, see-through iMac, and then the astonishingly small iBook.

Apple continued to blow customers away with industry-redefining products like the iPod and the iPhone. These were products straight out of science fiction. Never had a technology company seen rabid fans line up for days outside its stores to buy such expensive products.

The Apple brand is unmistakable and inescapable today. It's transformed the way most of us communicate, and as of this writing, it's number one on the Forbes 500, the single most profitable company in the world.

When trying to measure the love customers have for a brand, one American company that ranks close to both Apple and Disney is Harley-Davidson.

By this point, you won't be surprised to learn that William Harley was obsessed with trying to build a motorized bicycle at a young age. His fascination with the project was shared by his childhood friend, Arthur Davidson. The first motorized bicycle had been built in Germany only about six years before, made out of wood with a one-cylinder engine.

They knew they could do better.

Working out of a friend's machine shop on the north side of Milwaukee, the young pair spent two years working on the project just for fun. However, they had a serious deadline: Arthur had promised his brother Walter a ride on their new vehicle when he came to town for a wedding. It wasn't completed in time, and Walter was drawn into the project to help them build it.

When they finally managed to put together their first working motorcycle, it couldn't climb the hills around Milwaukee without being pedaled, so they went back to the drawing board.

They were concerned only with building a better motorcycle, not making money. In fact, only after a friend asked them to build him a motorcycle did they realize this might be a product people would actually want to buy. They sold a few, but spent all their spare time in the machine shop, working.

They weren't making enough money for the effort to be considered anything more than a hobby. They labored in the shadow of Henry Ford, who unveiled the model-A automobile in 1903. They continued to tinker, building several improved prototypes of single-cylinder motorcycles. Only after one of their vehicles won a 15-mile race in Chicago (with an average speed of about 50 mph) did sales increase enough to justify moving into a small factory of their own. After several years of obsessive work and a few dozen more sales, they were able to devote themselves fully to the company. In 1907 they doubled the size of their factory and grew to a dozen employees.

The craftsmanship and quality of Harley-Davidson motorcycles was unparalleled. They scored a perfect 1,000 at the 7th Annual Federation of American Motorcyclists Endurance and Reliability Contest. The reputation they earned didn't escape the attention of city police forces, who saw value in compact, motorized transport. They started placing orders.

Always innovating, always trying to make the best possible product, they introduced the two-cylinder motorcycle, the V-twin, in 1909.

They continued to win first place in races and hillclimb competitions, cementing their brand identity: serious, high-quality motorcycles for serious riders.

As the decades passed, their unwavering commitment to quality became legendary. Their logo, like the Coca-Cola logo, has only undergone the slightest tweaks over the company's nearly 120-year history, symbolizing their reliability and endurance. For many, Harley-Davidson is as outrageously stalwart a brand as America itself.

But what's more American, really, than Kentucky Fried Chicken?

No food-industry brand has more personality, nor is more iconically associated with an actual person, than KFC. Only Chef Boyardee comes close.

Harlan Sanders was another obsessed Outrageous Marketer.

He learned to cook before he could ride a bicycle. He bounced around various places working a variety of jobs for decades. He didn't find his mission until he was in his 40s. At the time, he was running a highway gas station in Kentucky.

What he loved doing was feeding people the delicious chicken recipe he'd spent a lifetime perfecting. He occasionally served it to hungry travelers who stopped at his gas station. The recipe was so good that, before long, word spread. People started to visit his store not to fuel up, but to order his chicken.

It was a magic recipe. He wowed customers with a product that was better than it had to be. He took the hint, and stopped serving gas and converted the filling station to a restaurant. His reputation for "finger lickin' good" chicken got him noticed. He was written up in the press. The governor made him an honorary Colonel.

But then the Interstate highway came through, shutting off most of the traffic to his old highway stop. He lost most of his business and had to auction off his restaurant at a loss.

At 66, he was a has-been local celebrity cook, living off social security. But he knew his recipe was great, and his mission was to feed people his amazing chicken. He was undaunted.

He convinced a friend to use the recipe at a restaurant in Utah, of all places. Again, word of mouth spread and several other restaurants asked for his recipe. He franchised it, making four cents for every chicken cooked with his recipe. He wanted to see it in more restaurants. So, he packed his pressure cookers in his car and traveled North America trying to sell his recipe. He visited hundreds of restaurants. If they let him, he would cook the entire restaurant staff a chicken dinner after they got off work. If they didn't think the chicken was "finger lickin' good," he would pack up and try again somewhere else. If they liked it, he would try to negotiate a franchise deal. Most of the restaurants, at first, rejected him. He often slept in his car on the road.

The Colonel knew quantity was the key to quality. After pitching restaurants for years, enjoying more of the word-of-mouth marketing he knew he could expect, he finally didn't have to drive to them anymore; they were coming to him. He had proven the quality of his product so thoroughly, he no longer had to sell it.

For nearly a decade, he and his wife mixed the secret recipe of 11 herbs and spices in their home and sent it themselves to the franchise restaurants. By 1963, there were more than six hundred of them, and the Sanders made a modest, comfortable living.

He sold the company when he was 73 to a businessman who would make a fortune serving the chicken out of branded Kentucky Fried Chicken restaurants. Part of the Colonel's deal was that he would be the restaurant's living mascot. His face would become the brand: the lovable character of the courtly Southern gentleman. And he lived the part to the hilt.

Long before "finger lickin' good" chicken, Charles Walgreen lost part of his middle finger working in a shoe factory when he was a teenager. He had wanted to play sports, but his injury left him only able to get a job at a drugstore in Dixon, Illinois, where he had a miserable experience. He learned a lot from his boss's failures.

He moved to Chicago, where a glutted drugstore market offered him the opportunity to work for several different pharmacists. With each one, he saw more failure and kept learning. The stores were cramped, dreary, and understocked. No attention was paid to customer service or value. Drugstores catered more to their own convenience than to that of their customers.

Though he arrived in Chicago without a penny in his pocket, eventually Charles was able to borrow $6,000 from one of his employers to buy a drugstore of his own, which took him years to pay off.

But now he could do it right.

He put in bright, pleasant lighting and widened the aisles, making customers feel welcome, even honored. He broadened and improved his offerings, including kitchen and bathroom products, which people didn't expect to see in a drugstore in the 1890s. What's more, he offered the items at bargain prices. This set him apart from not only every drugstore in town, but every department store too. It won him repeat customers and free word-of-mouth advertising.

Charles' most important innovation was a new attitude toward customers. He catered to their needs. He treated them like friends. He chatted with them. He filled their prescriptions personally and with only the finest compounds. Customers fell in love with Walgreens.

Not surprisingly, by 1920 Walgreens had 20 stores in the Chicago area. His convenient, welcoming stores were a sensation. Riding the wild economy of the decade, Walgreens grew to an astonishing 525 stores in major cities across the country by 1930. Charles was proud to proclaim he hired only people who were smarter than he was. His egoless approach to managing his teams led them to become loyal, lifetime employees dedicated to the success of the business.

Walgreens is a brand launched with a vision to treat customers well. Charles built a culture of people always looking for new ways to satisfy customers' needs. Over the decades, this brand identity can be codified in one word: convenience. The Walgreens culture has a deeply engrained mission to be outrageously convenient.

Every Walgreens store (there are almost 10,000 now) is located within five minutes of 76 percent of the U.S. population. They always prefer to build stores in convenient corner locations, with easily accessible parking. Only when they're forced by geography will they operate out of a mid-block address. And in those cases, as soon as a corner lot becomes available nearby, they'll buy it and move a few feet down the street in order to be in the more convenient space. They pioneered the delivery of pharmaceuticals. Now, customers no longer have to endure the indignity of announcing their strange rash in front of a bunch of strangers in a waiting room; they can get their prescription right at their door.

No matter what the brand is—family entertainment, computers, motorcycles, fried chicken or skin-rash cream—there's always an opportunity to live out the personality of the brand in the most outrageous way.

23

HOW IT CAN WORK FOR YOU

After spelling out what I did to build the *Onion* brand, as well as pointing to a few key examples from other brands, I offer these 13 insights, the principles of Outrageous Marketing:

1. Live your mission.

We all need to find the thing that lights a fire under us, the thing we were born to do. I found mine early, and by accident. Maybe you've already found yours. Maybe you're still looking. To live your mission you not only need to love what you do, you need to be compelled to do it. When you're in love with your work and it becomes your driving force, you'll do whatever it takes, and you'll be happy to do it. Success is in your mind, not on the balance sheet. I was successful when I was a kid making joke books that made my family laugh. I was successful when I was working sleepless nights at *The Onion*, desperate to fill the pages before the printing deadline. If you're not passionate about your work, it'll feel like an uphill battle. If you are, it'll feel like downhill skiing. When you live your mission and love what you do, you're already a success, no matter how much money you make.

2. Be obsessed.

People have always warned me about working obsessively. But I don't see the problem. I see only upside. I love what I do, and I love spending all my time doing it. It makes me happy. So, leave me alone and let me do it! People who are obsessed like me tend to get good at whatever it is they love doing. Steven Spielberg got good at making movies. Bill Gates got good at programming computers. When you work obsessively, you build skills, and in time you become a master. You become like Neo in *The Matrix*. You know the code of your craft, your profession, and your customers. You can bend the rules and innovate. You own your space. Someone like that can't be stopped from building a powerful brand.

3. Make people love you.

I was driven by my need for love, as are many other people in comedy. You may be driven by something else, but we all want love. If you think about potential customers and fans as potential friends or lovers, you'll start thinking about how to court them, woo them, and seduce them. Comedians make people laugh and feel good about themselves. Maybe your brand makes them feel something else positive. Maybe it solves a problem for them. Make it lovable. Turn on your charm and surprise them with quality. Be thoughtful and considerate of them. Overdeliver for them. Delight them. You know what I'm talking about. Go get 'em, tiger.

4. Focus on building fans, not profits.

Most companies are all about quarterly profits. I don't get it. I only ever concerned myself with pleasing my fans. Granted, I wasn't the business guy or the money guy. Those people are necessary to leverage what you do and sell it. But even before I had business partners I did the same thing. I worked for free. I did comedy as a hobby, an obsession. Whatever brand you're building, just worry about growing a fan base naturally. Do it cheaply. Do it in your spare time. Steal office supplies from your day job. If you love what you do, this will be easy. If you're an employee trying to promote someone else's company, sell the money people on a long-term plan to build fans that may not see a return on investment for a few years. They need to understand that sometimes acorns take more than a fiscal quarter to grow into oak trees.

5. Fire on all cylinders, and keep looking for new ones.

I always pursued the widest possible audience with my work because of my obsessive need to connect with people through comedy. I blanketed all media. I put *The Onion* out there in print, on radio, online, on video, in film and on merchandise. I put it out there in person, touring colleges with talks about *The Onion*. Whenever a new medium got invented, I put *The Onion* in it immediately. In retrospect, I see this was just smart branding. I was using the Ansoff Matrix before I knew what it was. This kind of obsessive brand diversification is a great way to reach more people and build more fans, of course, but it's also smart business. My push to get *The Onion* on every platform possible saved the company from financial ruin—twice. In 2002, when the Internet bubble burst, huge, multi-million-dollar Internet companies like boo.com and kozmo.com crashed and evaporated without a trace. But *The Onion* survived because 80 percent of our business was in print. The reverse happened in 2008 when the mortgage crisis hit the print-advertising economy hard. Just a few years later, *The Onion* would discontinue its print editions, but it survived because by then more than 80 percent of its business was digital. For non-media brands, the equivalent is to spread word of the brand in every medium, diversify retail channels, and pursue every possible ancillary product idea. You never know which one you might be counting on as a profit center in the future.

6. Find the best people.

Attract them by doing what they wish they were doing. I've always found that when I pursue my creative passions obsessively, like-minded people are drawn to me as if by gravity. People with the same obsession are compelled to join my effort. Soon I'm surrounded by a team. They work just as obsessively because they're inspired by my example. Those who don't will fall away fast. Soon I can step back and focus on the big picture while my team builds their skills and gets better. Eventually they become better and smarter than me. The only problem with this strategy is that at some point I'm the dumbest person in my company. But that's okay. This is how I find—more like cultivate—the best people, people who were not only born to do what they do, but people who are compelled to do it, who are just grateful for the opportunity to do it. This drives them to be the best.

7. Free your creatives.

Nobody likes a boss breathing down their neck. The best way to manage creatives is to tell them what you need and then leave them alone to do it. Don't give them office hours, don't give them unnecessary rules or requirements. Just free them to create. More companies are experimenting with "flextime," but that's a half measure. Cut the leash entirely. Empower your people to be like entrepreneurs inside your company. If they don't perform, lose them. Those who remain will perform beyond your wildest expectations. Freeing people is how you unleash their potential.

8. Don't accept conventional wisdom.

Just because everybody else is doing something doesn't mean that's the best way to do it. The only way to innovate is to try new things and see what works. Too many people are on autopilot. If you're going through life thinking you've already figured out the best way to do things, then you must not believe in the future. Because I guarantee in the future someone's going to figure out better, smarter and cheaper ways to do things. Marketing people are going to find better ways to be more sharable, lovable and profitable. Maybe that someone will be you. You'll never know if you don't try.

9. Serve the brand, not egos.

We're humans. We have egos. They're always going to be with us. At *The Onion*, I developed a system of content creation that eliminated ego as much as possible, and it's served the brand well. Egos are best eliminated in other parts of the company too. Unless I'm stroking the ego of someone on my team who's done a great job, I want ego eradicated from the office. In unhealthy organizations, too much time and energy is spent on people trying to fuel their egos. That time and energy needs to be redirected to fuel the brand. What would make it better? What can you do to sharpen its focus? What can you do to make people fall in love with it? What can you do to make it more outrageous?

10. Heighten your brand identity.

Define it, and then hone it. Figure out what your character archetype is. Harley-Davidson is the American biker. Disney is the friendly family entertainer. Apple is the future. *The Onion* is the bumbling authority. What's yours? Once you know it, riff on it. What are the things your fans would love the character of your brand to do?

11. Use quantity to achieve quality.

Most of the ideas we create are garbage. The best ideas come when you produce them in volume and pick the best ones. Come up with volumes of creative ideas. Let everyone in your organization cast a blind vote on them. Test them. Don't let your ego get in the way.

12. Do things that are press worthy.

If you want to get talked about in the media, don't just send out press releases; do things that are press worthy.

13. Embrace the outrageous.

Don't be afraid to stand out from the crowd. Embrace what makes your brand unique. The only rules are to serve your brand and give your customers what they want. Outside of that, it's an open field. Nothing is off limits. It's exciting to be a trailblazer. You might shock a few people, but you'll get the attention, and then the love, and then the respect of everybody else. I knew from an early age I wanted to imprint my thoughts on the culture in the form of jokes, make people laugh, and make the world a happier place. I would do anything to achieve it, no matter how outrageous, because it was the key to my emotional survival. Disney and Spielberg did the same to tell their stories. Colonel Sanders did it to sell fried chicken. Find your mission and live it. Be the most outrageous version of yourself as you can, and take a ride on the rocket ship.

24

I'M STILL WORKING

It's 3 a.m. again. My latest book is due to be uploaded to Amazon in two hours and I know I'm not going to make the deadline.

The problem is the last chapter. It's completely blank. I have nothing.

If I can't make some magic happen and fill this space with something—anything!—Amazon will go live with the rough draft I uploaded as a temp file the other day. It's a mess, unfinished, unorganized, and filled with private notes to myself. I'll be humiliated.

Amazon's self-publishing platform is run by robots. There's no way to reason with them. There's no way to bargain. There's no friendly person on a customer-service line waiting to give me just a little more time. When you set up a book for pre-order, it's a hard deadline.

What am I going to put here? After writing more than 25 books, you'd think I'd have it figured out by now.

It all rests on me, alone at my computer, bleary-eyed from editing and proofreading for more than 30 hours straight, trying desperately to get it done in time.

The strange thing is, as painful as this situation sounds—as painful as creating anything on a deadline always is—I'm still happy. I was happy chasing deadlines every week at *The Onion* too.

I'm happy because I'm in love with this life. It's the life I want. More importantly, it's the life I need. Not because I'm a masochist or thrill-seeker, but because this is who I am. Writing and creating and communicating is in my DNA. I love it.

My original business partner at *The Onion*, Pete, sometimes single-handedly sold all the ads necessary in a given week to make enough money for *The Onion* to continue publishing. I often joked with him that he could sell skis to a blind man. Pete taught me what he believed was the most important attribute of a great salesman: you have to love the product. And he loved *The Onion*.

I marveled at Pete's ability to sell. I never thought of myself as a salesman, so I couldn't imagine going out and meeting people and convincing them to buy advertising like Pete did. But I realize now that I *was* a salesman. I was selling to our other customer, the reader. And I loved the product too.

There are a lot of ways to succeed at getting a message out to the world. In this book, I provided examples from my life, and others, of my method. It's a method that comes from a deep emotional need to connect. That need is met by reaching out to people with love in order to find love. When they love me back, the Love Economy is good to me.

When your emotional needs are on the line, and your survival instincts are brought to bear, you'll stop at nothing to reach your goals. No matter whether I'm at *The Onion* or doing my comic strip or making a podcast or writing a book, this inner drive is always pushing me, always compelling me, and always making me strive until the breaking point to get my message out.

This inner drive gives me an intense level of commitment to quality. It forces me to find every avenue of exposure possible and exploit it. It educates me and turns me into a master creator. It makes me a compelling leader who attracts like-minded people to join my effort. Over time, it guides me to define and build a brand.

All these things together make me an unstoppable force, destined to succeed. I don't need a budget because it's just who I am. It's what I want to do with my time anyway. I'll find a way to do it, some way, some how. Because I have to. It's like breathing.

That's Outrageous Marketing.

ACKNOWLEDGMENTS

I owe much appreciation to the following people:

Everyone I employed or worked with or who employed me at *The Onion* over the years who made the experience central in my life—you know who you are; Mary Gardner and Ian Harris for their insights on marketing and business and how to articulate my thoughts on the subject; All the agents at Keppler Speakers Bureau, especially Dustin Jones, Theo Moll, John Truran, Chris Clifford, and Joel Gheesling, for exposing me to opportunities to tell my stories, and for encouraging me to write them down; Leah Harris, Kayal Rajendran, Mike Albanese and all the people at the Digital Summit, for inspiring me to write this book; All my friends and followers on social media who encouraged and supported me while I wrote the book; Rachel Reid for her inspiration, and for one day telling her story; Brooke Washington for her positivity, understanding, and support; Alyssa Haaganson and Ian Harris for their dedicated last-minute editing and proofing; Kenneth J, Artis for providing valuable details about important incidents in *The Onion*'s legal history; Daniel Greenberg for his invaluable book-publishing advice; Madeline Schmidt for her tireless work in both marketing and picking up groceries—this book would not have been possible or at least turned in on deadline without her help.

And for their superb marketing assistance, Salim Alam, Jason Andrews, Mary Williams Barber, Catherine Brinkman, David Calkins, Monica Carmean, Christy Devlin, Jared Dunne, Lindsay Ellis, Alan Epstein, Sarah Ervin, Matt Fischer, Madison Glimp, Josh Grant, Jake Gunst, Bobby Harris, Katie Healey, Ted Jacobs, Kate James, Doc Kane, O.Brian Kaufman, Hugh Kelly, Justin Kettle, JohnTom Knight, Radek Kocjan, Sarah Little, Sophia Loomis, Bill Loumpouridis, Julie Marchiano, Katie Mastropieri, Chris McNai, Jason Messina, Tim Mies, Grant Mulitz, Kayla Mulliniks, Jason Nawara, Dianne Nora, D.J. Paris, Daniel Parmet, Peter Parsons, Catherine Povinelli, Matt Prager, Robert Prorak, Gary Prusaitis, Emily Ramirez, Matthew Reeves, Luke Schneider, Eddie Shleyner, Eric Stassen, Erik Sternberge, Jen Syperski, Jim Taylor, Robert Torbett, Mark Toriski, Fidel Uribe, Erin Kay Van Pay, Ashley Vanove, Alexa Vaughn, Justin Vestal, John Walsh, Michael Williams, Patryk Wlodarski, and Julie Ziegler—I hope you all know how valuable you've been to the book's launch.

For the audiobook edition, Marcellus Hall, Keith Webster, Peter Hilleren, and Doug Rock for the inclusion of their voices or writing talents on the old radio sketches we produced when we were young. P.S. Mueller, Jay Rath, Todd Hanson, Michelle Loken for the Radio Pirates and *Onion Radio News* clips. Rich Dahm, Andrew Rohn, Brian Stack, Nancy Carell, Matt Spiegel, Rich Hutchman and Andrea Gall and Todd Hanson again for *The Comedy Castaways*. And thanks to Dandelion Benson for her unqualified support and bedazzlement at the sound of my voice.

SCOTT DIKKERS' BIG BOOK OF FAILURES

That's right—there's a hidden bonus chapter of this book! In it, I get a little more personal and tell the agonizing story of some of my biggest creative and financial disasters. I also reveal how I picked myself back up after my life fell apart.

To keep reading, just go here and sign up for my mailing list:

www.scottdikkers.com/outrageous/

Head over there now and sign up! It's free. You'll get sent to a page with the chapter on it.

If you're one of those people who hates reading things on a computer screen, I get it. After you sign up for the email list, you'll be taken to my website. Click the "contact" link at the bottom of the page. Send me a note letting me know you'd like a paper copy of the chapter. I'll drop it in the mail for you.

Thank you.

Made in the USA
Las Vegas, NV
02 September 2021